TRUE CRIME CASE HISTORIES
VOLUME 14

JASON NEAL

JASONNEALBOOKS.COM

Copyright © 2024 by Jason Neal
All rights reserved.

No part of this book may be reproduced in any form or by any electronic or mechanical means, including information storage and retrieval systems, without written permission from the author, except for the use of brief quotations in a book review.

Great effort and research have gone into the compilation of this material. It is the author's intention to represent the information within as accurately as possible. However, the author and publisher do not guarantee the accuracy of the text, graphics, and information presented. Any errors, omissions, or misinterpretations of this publication are not the responsibility of the author, copyright holder, or publisher. Although based on fact, some character names may have been changed, and/or scenes and dialogue may have been fictionalized. This publication is produced solely for informational and entertainment purposes and is not intended to hurt or defame anyone involved.

Cover images of:

Charles Rathbun: (top-left)

Melissa Turner: (top-right)

Robert Buell: (bottom-left)

Douglas Garland: (bottom-right)

More books by Jason Neal

Looking for more?? I am constantly adding new volumes of True Crime Case Histories. The series **can be read in any order**, and all books are available in paperback, hardcover, and audiobook.

Check out the complete series at:

https://amazon.com/author/jason-neal

All Jason Neal books are also available in **AudioBook format at Audible.com.** Enjoy a **Free Audiobook** when you signup for a 30-Day trial using this link:

https://geni.us/AudibleTrueCrime

FREE BONUS EBOOK FOR MY READERS

As my way of saying "Thank you" for downloading, I'm giving away a FREE True Crime e-book I think you'll enjoy.

https://TrueCrimeCaseHistories.com

Just visit the link above to let me know where to send your free book!

CONTENTS

Introduction	ix
1. The Castle Doctrine	1
2. The South Side Strangler	15
3. The Cosplay Cam Girl	33
4. Room 308	47
5. The Cape Coral Monster	63
6. A Bad Actor	77
7. The Frame-up	93
8. The City Planner	111
9. Death of a Cheerleader	131
10. Mother's Day	145
11. Collateral Damage	153
12. The Suitcase Killer	165
13. The Alabama Hatchet Murder *FREE BONUS CHAPTER*	183
Online Appendix	193
Also by Jason Neal	195
Free Bonus Book	197
Thank You!	199
About the Author	201

INTRODUCTION

If you've read the other books in my True Crime Case Histories series, you know that I always begin with a brief caution to my readers: True crime isn't for the faint of heart, and the stark reality of these stories can be profoundly disturbing. Oftentimes, true crime television shows or news stories can gloss over the gruesome parts, but in my books, I do my best to give you every detail, regardless of how unsettling they can be. I include these details not to sensationalize, but to provide readers with a deeper understanding of the killer's mind. Although it may be impossible for us to fully grasp their motives, the sheer magnitude of their depravity will compel you to keep reading.

Each story in my books requires hours of tedious research. I search through court records, old newspaper articles, police records, autopsy reports, and first-hand accounts. Although I may occasionally change a character's name or fictionalize bits of dialogue, these crimes actually happened to real people. Sadly, this is the world in which we live.

If you find the unsettling specifics of true crime too disturbing, this book may not be a good fit for you. However, if you're prepared for the raw and unfiltered reality, then let's begin.

Volume 14 of True Crime Case Histories highlights another twelve stories taking place over the past fifty years. Perhaps the most challenging aspect of writing true crime is discovering stories that my readers haven't already heard of. Given the saturation of true crime content in today's media, across television shows and podcasts, this task can seem nearly impossible. However, my greatest resource is my readers. Many of the stories in this volume were sent to me by readers like you. I rely on you to suggest story ideas that might have escaped the attention of major media. If you ever come across a lesser-known story that you believe deserves research, please don't hesitate to email it to me.

Lastly, please join my mailing list for discounts, updates, and a free e-book. You can sign up for that at:

TrueCrimeCaseHistories.com

Additional photos, videos, and documents pertaining to the cases in this volume can be found on the accompanying web page at:

TrueCrimeCaseHistories.com/vol14

Thanks again for reading, and I sincerely hope you gain some insight from this volume of True Crime Case Histories.

- Jason Neal

CHAPTER 1
THE CASTLE DOCTRINE

Little Falls, Minnesota, was a small town with a tight-knit population of just under 8,000, nestled on some of the northernmost banks of the Mississippi River. Sixty-four-year-old Byron Smith's Elm Street home, a secluded haven surrounded by towering pine trees, was just mere steps from the river's edge.

Smith lived alone and had never been married. A very private person by nature, many townspeople in Little Falls thought of him as a recluse who kept mostly to himself, often posting "keep out" signs at the entrance to his property. Others who knew Byron and his backstory of being a war hero and security expert thought of him as a friendly neighbor who just wanted to be by himself.

Byron Smith had spent his entire life around guns and could often be found in his backyard, shooting rounds into targets placed along his property. Yet, despite the distance separating him from his nearest neighbors, police often received complaints hinting at the ever-looming possibility of a stray bullet finding an unintended mark, possibly hitting a child playing at the nearby baseball complex.

Throughout his life, Byron Smith's job had kept him moving around, and by the time he had retired and inherited the home in Little Falls from his parents, he didn't have many friends nearby. Although he had originally grown up in Little Falls, most of his childhood friends had long since moved away.

Years earlier, Smith had served in the Air Force, including a tour in Vietnam. His exemplary service had earned him several medals and commendations, and he had also received electrical engineering training during his time in the military.

After leaving the Air Force, Smith transitioned to a position with Hughes Aerospace in California. While working, he simultaneously pursued an engineering degree at Cal Poly, juggling his job responsibilities with his studies.

Smith then moved on to work for the United States State Department, where he worked as a technical security engineer. This position afforded him the opportunity to travel the globe, undertaking assignments at various U.S. Embassies worldwide where he designed, installed, and monitored intricate security systems.

Smith traveled extensively to Bangkok, Cairo, Beijing, Moscow, and numerous other locations. As he rose through the ranks, he eventually found himself supervising teams of more than fifty employees. His primary responsibility was to safeguard U.S. Embassies against the threat of international espionage and terrorism.

This role demanded an exceptionally high level of security clearance, necessitating rigorous background checks and mental health screenings. Additionally, proficiency in surveillance techniques was essential to his duties.

In his late fifties, after decades with the State Department, Byron Smith finally retired to his small hometown but found it had changed drastically. Much to his dismay, he discovered that the once-charming small town had fallen prey to a pervasive wave of teenage drug use, as well as the theft and crime that goes along with it.

Smith struggled to accept that, after spending his whole life keeping bad people out of high-security places, he now had to protect his simple country home from teenagers using drugs.

During the six years since his retirement, Byron Smith's secluded home, nestled away from the road, had fallen victim to burglary on multiple occasions. While the thieves hadn't made off with anything of substantial value except for a few guns, the mere fact that someone had violated his privacy and rummaged through his possessions left him feeling disheartened.

Despite his extensive background in security, Smith lived in constant fear that a drug-addled teenager might attempt to break into his house while he was at home. To mitigate this anxiety, he instructed his neighbors to ring the doorbell twice in succession if they ever visited. This served as a signal that it was safe for him to open the door.

After each break-in, Smith bit his tongue and didn't report it to police, hoping they would eventually stop on their own. However, the break-ins just kept happening.

In October 2011, while Smith was away from his home, an intruder forcefully kicked in his door. Unlike previous incidents, this time the thief made off with items of both monetary and sentimental value. The stolen loot amounted to over ten thousand dollars, including an antique camera, valuable coins, a shotgun, electronics, a chainsaw, and four thousand dollars in cash. However, the loss cut deeper, as some items held profound personal significance, such as a watch awarded to his father for enduring captivity as a Prisoner of War in World War II and several medals earned by Smith himself during his service in Vietnam.

Fed up with the recurring burglaries, Smith finally acted and reported the break-in to the police. He also enlisted the help of a neighbor to assist with installing a security system in his house—something he had spent his life doing but never imagined he would need to do in his own home. Still, despite the added security measures, Smith continued to grapple with fear, haunted by the possibility of the intruders returning, potentially armed with the guns they had stolen.

Ironically, the installation of the video and audio monitoring system only worsened Smith's anxiety. He found himself frequently glued to the screens, anxiously scanning for any sign of intrusion. The fear of a drugged-out teenager breaking in weighed heavily on him, causing him to become increasingly apprehensive about leaving his home unattended.

Smith's paranoia reached such heights that he habitually wore a handgun holstered to his hip, even while inside the confines of his own home. Furthermore, he stockpiled a substantial supply of granola bars and water bottles in the basement, envisioning it as a potential refuge should the need arise to use it as a bunker.

―――

On Thanksgiving Day, 2012, Byron Smith received an invitation from a neighbor to join them for Thanksgiving dinner. However, Smith had become so reclusive that he hesitated to leave his house unattended, fearing another break-in. Aware that the intruder likely anticipated his absence on such a holiday, Smith made a deliberate decision to stay put, determined to thwart any potential burglary attempt.

While outside early on Thanksgiving morning, he saw a young girl he suspected had been behind the previous break-ins driving slowly past the driveway of his home. Later that morning, Byron Smith devised a cunning plan. He drove his truck out from his driveway and parked it in front of a neighbor's house, creating the illusion that he wasn't home.

Sneaking back through the woods to his house, he strategically positioned his reading chair between two bookcases in a shadowy corner of the basement, giving him a clear view of anyone descending the basement stairs. He then unscrewed all the lightbulbs throughout the house except for a dim reading light near his chair and placed a .22 caliber revolver and a Ruger Mini-14 rifle by his side.

Smith then turned on a digital audio recording device. As he sat in the dark, he recorded his thoughts and waited patiently for the intruders.

―――

While most families in Little Falls were sitting down for a turkey dinner, eighteen-year-old Haile Kifer and her seventeen-year-old cousin Nicholas Brady were looking for a house to break into. Despite their young age, the two teens had been breaking into homes throughout Little Falls to steal items they could sell to buy drugs.

Haile, a lifelong resident of Little Falls, was in her senior year of high school and excelled in sports while juggling multiple jobs in town. Despite being a role model for many, she had recently battled drug addiction. Similarly, her cousin Nicholas was well-liked in the community and earned a decent income working with his father's tree trimming business. Unfortunately, he had also faced struggles with substance abuse.

Smith's security cameras, hidden from view, picked up Nicholas Brady walking around the house just after noon on Thanksgiving, looking for an easy entry point.

Byron Smith sat in the dark and whispered to himself, "In your left eye."

Smith continued speaking into his digital recorder as if he were practicing a conversation he planned to have with his brother:

> "Stop by tomorrow, Bruce. No rush, but whenever's convenient. Park to the north. One hundred yards north of the corner, walk in from the west. I realize I don't have an appointment, but I would like to see one of the lawyers here."

Despite the outward appearance of random murmurs, Smith's whispered words were far from aimless: They were a deliberate rehearsal of the explanations and statements he intended to deliver to lawyers and law enforcement personnel following the execution of his plan.

Moments later, his audio recording picked up the sound of breaking glass on the main level of the house above him. He knew the intruder was now inside. Smith clicked off his reading light, sat silently, and waited patiently.

After twelve minutes of scouring Smith's home looking for something to steal, Nicholas Brady opened the basement door. Flicking the light switch on the wall, he was met with darkness. Slowly, Nicholas descended the stairs one step at a time.

As Nicholas came into view, Smith aimed his Ruger and unleashed two shots, striking Nicholas in the torso. Nicholas Brady tumbled down the remaining stairs, collapsed on the carpet below, and began bleeding out. Smith then approached Nicholas, standing over him. As Nicholas instinctively raised his hand in a futile attempt to shield himself, Smith fired once more, the bullet piercing through his finger before administering the fatal shot to his head. Smith then said to the dead boy, "You're dead."

Unfazed by the harrowing events, Smith methodically continued his plan, all while his audio device captured the eerie scene. He made taunting remarks to the boy's body as he carefully spread out a green camouflage tarp on the floor and moved Nicholas' lifeless body onto it. With grim determination, he dragged the body into another room within the basement, concealing it from view. He then used a throw rug to cover the blood and brain matter that had soiled his carpet at the bottom of the stairs.

As Nicholas had tumbled down the stairs, his shoes had flown off his feet and now lay abandoned on the basement floor. Smith, with a quiet sense of purpose, retrieved the sneakers and tucked them neatly under his reading chair before walking back upstairs.

Fifteen minutes later, Smith's realization struck: Nicholas wasn't alone. As he faintly heard a female voice calling out, "Nick?" through the broken bedroom window, Smith stealthily descended the basement stairs again, reloaded his rifle, and settled back into the shadowy reading chair. With unwavering resolve, he remained prepared for the second intruder.

Smith sat in silence as Haile Kifer quietly descended the stairs. Again, without even seeing Haile's face or if she was armed, Smith shot her in the back.

Haile screamed as she tumbled down the stairs. With Haile injured at the bottom of the stairs, Smith tried to shoot again, but his rifle jammed, "Oh, sorry about that," he said. Smith would later claim that Haile had laughed at him because his gun jammed, but no laughter was caught on his recording device—only screams and pleas.

As Haile screamed, "No, no!" Smith grabbed his revolver, shot her again, and screamed, "You're dying! Bitch!" When he saw Haile was still squirming on the rug at the bottom of the stairs, he continued shooting. One shot went through her left eye, as he had mentioned in an earlier recording. After six shots, Haile was still gurgling and clinging to life. Smith verbally berated her before putting his revolver to her chin, aiming up toward her cranium, and pulling the trigger.

Byron Smith then dragged Haile's bullet-riddled body into the side room and piled her on top of her dead cousin's body.

For hours after the killings, Byron Smith sat isolated in his basement, whispering into his digital audio recorder, chastising the teens he killed, practicing what he would tell police, rationalizing his actions, and letting his thoughts wander aimlessly.

> "Cute. I'm sure she thought she was a real pro."

> "No rush but, you know, when it's convenient for you. ... I feel a little safer. ... I feel totally safe. I'm still shaking a bit."

> "It's all fun… cool… exciting, and highly profitable until somebody kills you."

> "I was doing my civic duty. ... They messed with the wrong person, I had to do it."

> "They weren't human. I don't see them as human."

> "I am not a bleeding-heart liberal. I felt like I was cleaning up a mess. Not like spilled food. Not like vomit. Not even like diarrhea. The worst mess possible."

> "Because I try to be a decent person, they think I'm a patsy. I'm a sucker. They think I'm there for them to take advantage of."

> "I refuse to live with that level of fear in my life."

Smith continued to ramble about how, if the intruders had been caught and prosecuted, they would have been released after only six months of jail time, saying, "I cannot live like that. I cannot have that chewing on me forever."

At the end of the recording, he rambled to himself about an imaginary death threat, saying, "I gave you a copy of a death threat. I expect you to do something about it."

Not wanting to bother police during the holidays, Byron Smith sat with the two dead bodies in his basement until the next day before contacting anyone.

Initially, he called a neighbor and asked him to call a lawyer, but he wouldn't tell him why. Only saying, "I blew the top off the break-ins down here." The friend called around, but it was the day after Thanksgiving, and every law office in town was closed. Smith then asked the friend to contact the police and have them send a Sergeant to his house.

When the Morrison County Sheriff's Department arrived at Smith's residence, they initially believed they were investigating a routine break-in. However, they knew something was wrong when Smith greeted them outside his home with his hands raised in surrender.

Smith then told them there had been another break-in, led them into the house, and showed them the point of entry—the broken window in his bedroom.

However, upon accompanying Smith to the basement, officers were confronted with a chilling sight: blood stains smeared across the stairwell walls, and a pool of blood gathered at the foot of the stairs. Instantly, they realized the situation was far more sinister than they had anticipated.

Smith then led officers to a closed door in the basement, pointed to it, and said, "The bodies are behind here."

When officers saw the bodies of the two popular high school students, they immediately took Byron Smith into custody and charged him with second-degree murder.

Smith wasted no time and calmly told investigators the entire story.

> "I was in the basement in my favorite reading chair reading a paperback, and I see a shadow go past the picture window. And then somebody's rattling the basement door trying to get in. But it's also locked and deadbolted."

Smith told investigators that he watched on his newly installed surveillance cameras as two intruders jiggled door handles and put their faces up to his windows to look inside. He said he then heard a window break, and he panicked and grabbed his two guns.

> "So I'm sitting there and I hear the steps coming down the hallway, and come down the stairs. These are people who have stolen my guns. I figured they're willing to use guns if they steal guns. I decided that I've got a choice of either shooting or being shot."

> "I'm not gonna wait until she shows it. I knew that they were both gun thieves. As far as I was concerned, they were totally dangerous."

> "After I shot him, I sat down in this chair, and I was just tingling—adrenaline. I hate adrenaline. And my blood was pounding in my ears, and I just wanted to calm down more than anything else."

> "And I hear more footsteps coming down the hallway, and somebody else starts down the stairs. I just couldn't think. I didn't think. I wasn't thinking. I was just… they're ganging up on me. So I killed her, too."

Smith claimed that when he positioned the revolver under Haile's chin and aimed up toward her cranium, it was a mercy killing, saying, "I gave her a good clean finishing shot. She gave out the death twitch."

When asked why he didn't immediately call the police, he said, "Just because my Thanksgiving's screwed up, I don't need to screw up yours."

Toxicology reports later revealed that Haile Kifer had both marijuana and the chemical components of cough medicine in her system. The substances were present at levels sufficient to cause intoxication and potentially induce hallucinations.

In his mind, Byron Smith had justified the lives he had taken. Even though the two teenagers weren't armed, he believed he had the right to protect himself inside his own home.

———

The Castle Doctrine is a legal principle in many jurisdictions that allows individuals to use force, including deadly force if necessary, to defend their homes, property, or sometimes their vehicles against intruders or attackers. The doctrine is based on the idea that individuals have the right to protect themselves and their homes from imminent threat or harm without the obligation to retreat. In essence, it gives individuals the legal right to defend their "castle" from intruders without fear of prosecution under certain circumstances. However, the specifics of the Castle Doctrine vary from state to state and, in most states, exclude the use of excessive force.

Byron Smith's case was very controversial in Minnesota. Many believed Smith had every right to protect himself within his own home. Others, however, believed he could have handled matters in another manner that didn't involve shooting two unarmed teenagers nine times.

Minnesota prosecutors contended that Byron Smith had overstepped boundaries. They argued that Smith's actions did not constitute self-defense; rather, he had meticulously set a trap and resorted to excessive force. Smith had intentionally concealed his truck that morning to entice Haile and Nicholas to his home. Furthermore, he had laid in wait as if he were hunting deer and fired upon them without certainty of any physical threat. Most concerning was his repeated firing into their heads at point-blank range, even after realizing they were unarmed and no longer posed a threat.

Smith's trial began on April 21st, 2014, and concluded after just a few days, with the jury beginning deliberations on April 29th. Astonishingly, it took the jury a mere three hours to reach a verdict. Byron David Smith was found guilty on two counts of first-degree murder and received a life sentence in prison without the possibility of parole.

One juror commented,

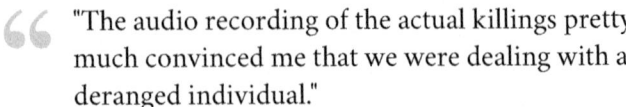
> "The audio recording of the actual killings pretty much convinced me that we were dealing with a deranged individual."

Despite Smith's lawyers filing an appeal to the Minnesota Supreme Court, the previous ruling was upheld. This was a decision that a Federal Appeals Court also affirmed.

On November 20th, 2020, nearly eight years after the Thanksgiving Day killings, Smith lodged an appeal with the Supreme Court of the United States. However, his appeal was ultimately denied on March 22, 2021.

The jury of public opinion is still divided on the case of Byron Smith. Social media pages have emerged advocating for Smith's freedom, with one Facebook page dubbing him a hero. Commenters on the page defended Smith's actions, describing Haile and Nicholas as troublemakers and suggesting that the tragedy could have been avoided if they had just stayed home. Conversely, other commenters condemned Smith as a cold-blooded murderer and urged for his continued incarceration. Despite conflicting opinions, jurors unequivocally labeled Smith as a murderer.

CHAPTER 2
THE SOUTH SIDE STRANGLER

The morning of September 19, 1987, dawned crisp and clear over Richmond, Virginia's affluent South Side neighborhood. Families eased into another relaxed Saturday as the last vestiges of summer still lingered in the air. Joggers took to tree-lined streets while others headed off to the farmer's market. Afternoon barbecues and pool gatherings were sure to come.

Unfortunately, the languid sense of security would soon be shattered after a phone call to Richmond Police.

Arnold Ellis returned home shortly after 1:00 a.m. after a Friday night spent with friends, only to spot an unfamiliar white car parked in front of his house. Paying it little mind, he retired for the night. However, when he woke the next morning and discovered the car was still there, his curiosity was piqued. Venturing out to the sidewalk, Arnold noticed the car was running. It had apparently been running all night, yet its owner was nowhere in sight. Concerned, he contacted the police to report the abandoned vehicle.

When police arrived and checked the registration on the little Renault Alliance, they found that it belonged to thirty-five-year-old Debbie Davis.

Debbie Davis lived in a ground-floor apartment of a large brick apartment building on Devonshire Street, just a block from where her car was found.

After numerous unanswered knocks on the door, officers were greeted by a neighbor who identified herself as Debbie's landlord. Concerned for her tenant's safety, the woman promptly provided a key and gave permission for the officers to enter Debbie's apartment.

Officers made their way through the tidy apartment, but when they reached the back bedroom, they were confronted with a grim and unsettling sight.

Debbie Davis lay face-down on the bed with her head partially hanging off the side of the mattress. She was nude from the waist up, wearing only cutoff jean shorts. She had been brutally raped and strangled.

Her right arm was bound tightly behind her back with bootlaces, while her left arm was tied beneath her. Two socks had been tied together tightly around her neck. Then, using a sixteen-inch metal vacuum cleaner extension tube, her killer had twisted it within the socks like a tourniquet.

The device had been used to slowly strangle her. Ruptures in the capillaries of her eyes indicated she had endured prolonged torture. The killer had twisted the tube, strangling her to the brink of death only to release the pressure, rape her again, and continue the process over again. It was apparent that the killer had repeated the process over and over again, possibly spending hours in her home.

The autopsy concluded Davis had been raped both vaginally and anally during the lengthy assault. Two large deposits of uncontaminated seminal fluid from her killer were left on the bedsheets, indicating he had masturbated repeatedly during the assault. It was clear the killer had derived sexual satisfaction from her suffering.

Investigators determined the killer had propped up an outside rocking chair beneath an open kitchen window and climbed, undetected, over the sink without disturbing any items around it. It was obvious he was agile and athletic and most likely had experience with break-ins.

The killer came prepared, likely wearing gloves to avoid leaving fingerprints behind. The only evidence recovered by investigators were two hairs and the semen on the sheets.

Debbie Davis had worked for Richmond's Style Magazine and was last seen the night before. She and several coworkers had gone to a comedy club to see the stand-up routine of Saturday Night Live's Dana Carvey. After learning of Debbie's brutal killing, Style Magazine's management offered a $10,000 reward for any information leading to the capture of her killer, but the sadistic monster was just getting started.

Dr. Susan Hellams was a respected neurosurgeon at the Medical College of Virginia. Before moving to Richmond, she met her husband, Marcel Slag, while working in Paris.

Two weeks after the murder of Debbie Davis, Marcel Slag arrived home after working late. As he entered their home, Marcel heard noises upstairs, assumed he'd awoken his wife, and quietly showered. However, when he got out of the shower, he soon discovered Susan's partially nude body on the floor, hanging halfway out of their closet. The noises he heard upstairs were likely his wife's last moments with her killer.

When Marcel found Susan, her skirt was bunched up around her waist and her hands were bound behind her back with an electrical cord. Two leather belts were used to kill her—a red one was pulled taut around her neck, and a black one attached to it had been used as a makeshift leash to strangle her. Blood covered her badly beaten face. Although her body still felt warm, Marcel knew she was dead when he dialed 911.

Investigators quickly determined that the murders of Susan Hellams and Debbie Davis were committed by the same person. The two crime scenes were located within a mile of each other. Moreover, the killer employed strikingly similar strangulation techniques in both homicides, further reinforcing the connection between the two cases.

The killer demonstrated remarkable agility and strength at both crime scenes. As with the previous murder, the perpetrator had gained entry to the house by scaling a wooden fence adjacent to the property, then used a cutting tool to slice through an upstairs window screen. From this precarious position, he was able to lift himself up and climb through the window.

As with the previous murder, investigators found minimal evidence inside the house, with the exception of semen discovered near Dr. Hellams' body. Additionally, the killer had left behind an open container of Vaseline on the exterior windowsill.

The murder method was also comparable to the previous case. Like Debbie Davis, Dr. Hellams had been slowly and systematically strangled. The killer had repeatedly choked her and then released the pressure, only to resume strangling her. Each time Dr. Hellams lost consciousness, the killer would stop long enough for her to regain awareness, then continue the cycle of choking and releasing until she ultimately died.

Given the striking similarities in the modus operandi and the short timeframe between the two gruesome murders, investigators had no doubt they were facing a serial killer. The consistent use of strangulation, the killer's impressive physical prowess in entering the homes, and the presence of seminal fluid at both crime scenes pointed to a single killer responsible for the heinous acts.

Faced with limited evidence and no clear suspect, investigators from the Richmond Police Department shifted their focus to identifying any potential connections between the two victims, Susan Hellams and Debbie Davis. By exploring their backgrounds, relationships, and daily routines, detectives hoped to uncover a common thread that might lead them closer to the killer.

Investigators soon discovered a link between the two crime scenes and Cloverfield Mall. They learned that victim Debbie Davis had been employed part-time at the mall's Waldenbooks store. Furthermore, detectives were able to determine that the jar of Vaseline found at the scene of Susan Hellams' murder had been purchased from a drugstore located within the same shopping center. These connections to Cloverfield Mall provided a promising lead for investigators to pursue as they worked to identify the serial killer.

A thorough examination of customer receipts from Waldenbooks revealed a crucial connection between the two victims. Records showed that Dr. Hellams had purchased a book directly from Debbie Davis at the store just weeks before both women were murdered. This discovery led investigators to suspect that the killer might have been using Cloverfield Mall as a hunting ground to select his targets. The theory suggested that the killer could have observed the interactions between Davis and her customers, such as Dr. Hellams, and then chosen his victims based on these encounters. Armed with this new information, investigators focused their efforts on identifying potential suspects with ties to the mall.

Despite the promising lead connecting the victims to Cloverfield Mall, investigators faced a daunting challenge: The shopping center was one of the most popular in the region, with a daily influx of thousands of visitors. Attempting to identify the killer based solely on his potential presence at the mall seemed like an insurmountable task. With limited resources and no further evidence, detectives struggled to make progress in the case. Tragically, their efforts were not enough to prevent the killer from claiming another life just seven weeks later, leaving the community in fear of the seemingly unstoppable serial murderer.

Diane Cho, a brilliant fifteen-year-old student, was thriving in her freshman year at Manchester High School. With her exceptional academic performance, she had already set her sights on attending medical school after graduation. Diane and her family lived in the Chesterfield Village Apartments, located in close proximity to Cloverfield Mall. The shopping center served as a popular weekend hangout spot for Diane and her fellow classmates, providing a convenient location for socializing and leisure activities.

Diane and her family were recent immigrants from Korea, having settled in Richmond just five months prior. Despite the challenges of adjusting to a new country and language, Diane's parents had managed to establish a small convenience store. However, their limited English proficiency made navigating daily life and running the business difficult. Diane, who had quickly adapted and become fluent in English, played a crucial role in supporting her family. She acted as a translator and facilitator, assisting her parents with every aspect of their lives, from communicating with customers at the store to handling essential paperwork and appointments.

In recent weeks, Diane had shared a disturbing concern with her closest friends. She confessed that she had noticed a man at Cloverfield Mall who seemed to be following her, and the unsettling experience had begun to haunt her dreams. Diane's friends, while sympathetic, had no idea that her nightmares were a chilling premonition of the horror that awaited her.

―――――

On a Saturday night in late November 1987, Diane Cho's mother gave her a haircut at around 9:00 p.m. before retiring for the night at approximately midnight.

The following morning, Diane's parents left the apartment early to run some errands before the family's planned church attendance that afternoon. They left Diane and her younger brother, Roman, at home by themselves, expecting to return in time for church.

Diane's parents returned home just after 2:00 p.m., and Diane was still in her bedroom. Roman told his parents he hadn't seen his sister all day, explaining that he didn't want to disturb her if she wanted to sleep late.

Concerned, Mrs. Cho entered Diane's bedroom and walked into a horrifying scene. Diane lay face-down on her bed with a rope tightly wound around her neck. Her face had turned a deep purple color, and the bedroom window was open. Roman, being the only family member proficient in English, immediately dialed 911. When the emergency operator instructed him to perform CPR, Roman solemnly replied, "It's too late. She's dead."

Upon arriving at the scene, detectives quickly noticed the striking similarities between Diane Cho's murder and the previous two killings. The perpetrator had employed a rope to repeatedly choke Diane, bringing her to the brink of unconsciousness before releasing the pressure, only to start the process again. As with the other victims, evidence suggested that the killer had masturbated while watching Diane's slow and agonizing death. Diane had also been subjected to a brutal sexual assault. The murderer had used the same distinct arrangement of ligatures as seen in the prior cases, leaving no doubt in the investigators' minds that they were dealing with a serial killer who had claimed yet another innocent life.

The killer's modus operandi remained consistent with the previous murders: He had carefully removed a window screen and entered the apartment through the opening, just as he had done in the other cases. This time, however, the killer's actions took on a new level of audacity and cruelty. He had brutally ended the life of a young, innocent girl while her unsuspecting family members slept just a short distance away in their own bedrooms.

Consistent with the previous crime scenes, the killer was meticulous in avoiding leaving any fingerprints that could be used to identify him. However, he had once again left behind vital biological evidence in the form of semen and a single pubic hair on Diane's body.

As detectives delved into Diane's background, interviewing her friends and family, they uncovered a chilling connection to Cloverfield Mall and the unsettling presence of a stalker. Diane's close friend, Jenny, provided a crucial piece of information to the police. She recounted an incident at the mall when she and Diane were purchasing tickets to watch the movie *The Princess Bride*. Jenny described a man who had stared at them intensely, his gaze filled with a disturbing emptiness. She emphasized that the man's eyes were the coldest she had ever encountered, devoid of any warmth or humanity.

A mere five days after the tragic murder of Diane Cho, and approximately 100 miles north of Richmond, forty-four-year-old Susan Tucker was preparing her townhome in Arlington, Virginia, for sale. Susan and her husband, Reggie, were in the process of relocating to his native country of Wales, and getting their current residence ready for the market was a crucial step in their plans.

Reggie had already gone to Wales, while Susan remained in Arlington to prepare their townhome for sale. The couple spoke on the phone daily during this time apart. However, Reggie noticed that Susan's calls had stopped suddenly. Growing concerned, he repeatedly tried to reach her over the next few days, but his calls went unanswered.

A neighbor also noticed something unusual at the Tucker residence. Despite the cold November weather, one of the townhome's windows had been left wide open for several days. Worried about Susan's well-being, the neighbor approached the front door. However, she was immediately struck by a horrible odor coming from the open window. The neighbor knew something wasn't right and called the police.

When officers arrived at the scene, they also noticed the strong smell and entered the townhome to investigate further. They discovered a woman's purse lying on the floor just inside the entrance, its contents scattered about, indicating potential signs of a struggle.

The officers followed the foul smell to the couple's bedroom, where they made a grim discovery. Susan Tucker's severely decomposed body lay face-down on the bed, her hands bound behind her back with nylon rope. A separate rope was tightly wound around her neck, with an additional length extending from the neck ligature to her restrained hands. The configuration of ropes was eerily similar to the bindings used in the previous victims' murders. The killer had once again used the sadistic technique of repeatedly tightening the rope to choke Susan to the brink of death, only to release the pressure momentarily before starting the torturous cycle again.

The killer had gained access through a basement window, using a washing machine as a step to enter the residence. Once inside, the killer took great care to avoid leaving any footprints behind, meticulously cleaning the areas where he had stepped. As with the previous crime scenes, no fingerprints were discovered anywhere in the house, despite clear indications that the intruder had spent a considerable amount of time there. The home had been thoroughly ransacked, and he had even made himself a snack at one point.

Although the murder happened more than 100 miles away, Arlington's Detective Joe Horgas believed the methodology of the killer was the same as the murders in Richmond. Richmond detectives, however, weren't so sure. Eventually, the semen and pubic hair evidence left behind would prove the murders were all done by the same killer.

Detective Horgas also remembered another murder that had strong similarities. Years earlier, in January 1984, an Arlington attorney named Carolyn Hamm was found murdered in her garage. Carolyn Hamm was murdered only a few blocks from Susan Tucker, and like the others, she had been strangled using the same configuration of ligatures. There was only one problem: Carolyn Hamm's killer was already behind bars.

Back in 1983 and 1984, Arlington had been terrorized by an unidentified serial rapist dubbed "The Masked Rapist." In January, after Carolyn Hamm was murdered, two people came forward claiming to have seen a man named David Vasquez in the neighborhood on the night of the murder.

Vasquez, a frail-looking man with the intelligence level of a third-grader, quickly became the prime suspect.

Despite the lack of fingerprints, inconsistent hair evidence, and a mismatch between the blood type of the semen found on Carolyn Hamm's body and Vasquez's blood type, the police remained convinced of his guilt. After a lengthy fourteen-hour interrogation and a polygraph test, Vasquez, a quiet man with an IQ of 70, confessed to second-degree murder and burglary to avoid the possibility of receiving the death penalty. As a result, David Vasquez was sentenced to thirty-five years in prison with the chance of parole after serving five and a half years.

After Vasquez's arrest, the string of unsolved rapes in the Arlington area had stopped. The timing convinced prosecutors that Vasquez was indeed the "Masked Rapist" responsible for Hamm's death and they had imprisoned the right man. Sadly, however, the cessation was merely a tragic coincidence.

Unbeknownst to authorities, the real Masked Rapist and killer had been arrested just five days after Carolyn Hamm's murder for unrelated counts of burglary and larceny. Four years later, the killer was released back on the streets of Richmond and strangling women in their homes.

Detective Horgas from Arlington noticed striking similarities between the murders of Susan Tucker and Carolyn Hamm. The two victims lived just a few blocks apart, and in both cases, the killer had demonstrated athletic prowess by crawling through open windows and intelligence by meticulously avoiding leaving fingerprints. However, the most unsettling parallel was the manner in which the perpetrator strangled the women and left behind semen at the crime scenes.

Detective Horgas visited David Vasquez in prison, wondering if maybe he had worked with a partner during the rapes and murder. However, after hours of speaking with Vasquez, Horgas was convinced that he knew nothing of the murder of Carolyn Hamm. He couldn't answer even the most basic questions about the crime for which he was imprisoned.

Detective Horgas sent the semen sample collected from Susan Tucker's crime scene to a specialized laboratory in New York that focused on the emerging field of DNA extraction. As he awaited the results, Horgas reached out to the FBI's Behavioral Science Unit, seeking assistance in creating a profile of the killer.

The FBI provided a potential profile, suggesting that he was likely between the ages of 21 and 30, a loner, and had a history of breaking and entering. They also believed that the perpetrator probably had an extensive criminal record, which may have begun with arson. Furthermore, the FBI suggested that the killer likely resided in close proximity to the crime scenes.

Following Detective Horgas' investigation, Richmond authorities were now persuaded that his theory was correct. They believed that, despite the 100-mile distance between the two cities, they were likely dealing with the same killer in both Richmond and Arlington.

As a veteran law enforcement officer who had spent his entire career in Arlington County, Detective Horgas was familiar with many local criminals. When the FBI proposed that the killer likely lived in the area and had a history of arson, Horgas began to recall names of individuals he had arrested over the years. One particular juvenile offender who came to mind was Timmy Spencer, who Horgas had encountered years earlier.

Twenty-five-year-old Timothy Wilson Spencer was no longer a juvenile, and Horgas remembered Spencer as a troublemaker. Even as a child, he had a steady string of offenses —usually petty crimes and larceny. One crime, however, stood out in Horgas' mind. As a teenager, Horgas had arrested Spencer for setting fire to his mother's car.

When Horgas checked the police database to see what Spencer had been up to in his adult life, he realized he hadn't changed much. In recent years he had been arrested for breaking and entering, larceny, and grand theft.

Spencer was apprehended shortly after the Arlington rapes and the murder of Carolyn Hamm. Following his arrest, he served a four-year prison sentence before being released on parole and placed in a halfway house in Richmond.

Spencer had been placed in the Richmond halfway house mere weeks before the murders of Debbie Davis, Susan Hellams, Diane Cho, and Susan Tucker. Notably, the halfway house was within walking distance of both Debbie Davis and Susan Hellams' homes.

Despite Susan Tucker's murder having taken place 100 miles away in Arlington, it was noted Timothy Spencer had been granted temporary leave from the halfway house at the time of the crime. He was in Arlington visiting his mother, who lived less than a mile from Susan Tucker's location.

While the evidence connecting Timothy Spencer to the murders was circumstantial, he fit the FBI's profile of the killer perfectly. As investigators awaited the DNA results from Susan Tucker's crime scene, which was still being processed in New York, they began surveillance on Spencer. During this surveillance, they noticed he spent a significant amount of time at Cloverfield Mall.

Investigators realized that if they could present sufficiently compelling evidence to a grand jury, they could secure an arrest warrant for Timothy Spencer. This arrest warrant would allow them to obtain a DNA sample from him, which could then be compared to the DNA profile of Susan Tucker's assailant. On January 20, 1988, a grand jury in Arlington County indicted Timothy Spencer on charges of burglary, rape, and murder in connection with the death of Susan Tucker.

Without delay, officers obtained blood and hair samples from Spencer and dispatched them to a laboratory in New York for comparison with the profile obtained from the crime scene of Susan Tucker.

When confronted with the charges, Timothy Spencer insisted that he had never encountered Susan Tucker and claimed that he had rarely left his mother's home during his time in Arlington. Furthermore, when questioned by Richmond Police, Spencer denied any involvement in the murders of Debbie Davis, Dr. Susan Hellams, and Diane Cho.

With Spencer's refusal to confess, investigators pinned their hopes on the DNA evidence, which at the time had never been used in the United States to secure a murder conviction.

Just a year prior, DNA evidence had been instrumental in securing the first-ever murder conviction worldwide, involving a baker from the UK found guilty of killing two teenage girls. With this groundbreaking precedent in mind, investigators anxiously awaited the results.

Six weeks later, the outcome arrived: Timothy Wilson Spencer's DNA profile unequivocally matched that of the semen found at Susan Tucker's crime scene. The likelihood of the DNA belonging to anyone other than Timothy Spencer was an astonishing 1 in 705,000,000.

―――

Timothy Spencer stood trial on July 11, 1989, for the rape and murder of Susan Tucker.

Despite efforts by his defense team to cast doubt on the credibility of the new scientific method, they found themselves with little ground to stand on against its undeniable validity. Coupled with Spencer's inability to provide an alibi and the presence of other incriminating evidence, such as hair samples and glass shards on his clothing, the jury harbored no uncertainty.

On July 11, 1988, Timothy Wilson Spencer was found guilty of Susan Tucker's murder and sentenced to death.

Following the trial, a chain reaction ensued as Richmond Police, equipped with DNA samples from their own investigations into the murders of Debbie Davis, Dr. Susan Hellams, and Diane Cho, swiftly obtained guilty verdicts in each case. Consequently, three more death sentences were handed down.

In a historic milestone, Spencer secured his place as the first serial killer in the United States to be convicted using DNA evidence, marking a pivotal moment in forensic science and criminal justice.

The following year brought about another significant development when David Vasquez became the first person to be exonerated due to DNA evidence. After serving five years for a crime he didn't commit, Vasquez was finally released from prison.

In total, Timothy Spencer was implicated in the murders of five women and considered the primary suspect in the Masked Rapists spree that plagued Arlington County, although he was never formally tried for these crimes.

Following his convictions, Spencer appealed his sentences. Each appeal was unsuccessful as the sentences were ultimately upheld by the Virginia Supreme Court.

On April 27th, 1994, Timothy Spencer met his fate in Virginia's electric chair. He was pronounced dead at 11:13 p.m., opting not to deliver a final statement.

The aftermath of Timothy Spencer's crimes continues to affect the families of his victims to this day.

Debbie Davis' tragic murder is still vividly remembered by those at Style Weekly, prompting the magazine to publish a comprehensive series on the case in 2018, marking the 30th anniversary of Spencer's conviction.

Dr. Susan Hellams is fondly remembered by her former husband, Marcel, and colleagues at the Medical College of Virginia for her compassionate caregiving.

Diane Cho's mother, who resides in Richmond, mourns her daughter daily, especially as many cherished photos were confiscated as evidence by Arlington Police and never returned.

Reggie, Susan Tucker's former husband, relocated to Canada after struggling with depression for years following her death. Despite the loss of two wives, he has found peace in retirement.

Timothy Spencer's crimes had a profound impact on Virginia, unsettling the Southern Richmond communities. Yet, they spurred progress in criminal justice, notably through the widespread use of DNA profiling, which has improved law enforcement's ability to catch criminals and prove innocence.

CHAPTER 3
THE COSPLAY CAM GIRL

Melissa Turner, born in 1992, spent her childhood in South Carolina and Florida, enjoying a typical middle-class upbringing. As a young teenager, she developed an interest in horror movies and cosplay, immersing herself in the world of fictional characters through elaborate costumes.

However, Melissa struggled with her weight during her teenage years, reaching 250 pounds by the time she graduated high school. The weight gain significantly impacted her self-esteem, causing her to withdraw from the cosplay community out of shame and embarrassment about her appearance.

As she entered her early twenties, Melissa found herself deeply dissatisfied with her life. Despite successfully earning an associate's degree in small business, she struggled to find employment that would validate her educational efforts. This lack of job prospects, combined with her ongoing struggle with weight and self-image, left her feeling disillusioned.

On top of her weight struggles, Melissa was burdened with over $26,000 in student loan debt, further exacerbating her challenges. Plagued by pervasive feelings of depression across various aspects of her life, Melissa reached a pivotal moment of realization. It was then that she resolved to take decisive action to turn her situation around.

It was a moment of reckoning for Melissa as she summoned her courage to confront her challenges head-on. Embarking on a transformative journey, she overhauled her diet and lifestyle. She gained a deeper understanding of health and nutrition by immersing herself in a wealth of knowledge from blogs, forums, and articles.

Through unwavering determination, Melissa achieved a remarkable feat and shed an astounding 90 pounds within the span of two years, going from 250 pounds in 2011 to a trim 160 pounds by 2013. While the physical transformation was evident, the true significance lay in her newfound self-love and happiness. This journey revitalized Melissa's spirit, instilling within her a renewed sense of joy and self-acceptance.

In 2013, Melissa formed a close bond with a man she had met online which eventually blossomed into a romantic relationship, marking her first serious commitment. Concurrently, Melissa decided to pursue her passion for special effects and makeup artistry, seeking professional training to hone her skills.

As her confidence grew, Melissa embraced her love for cosplay once again, dressing up as her favorite characters. She approached this hobby with renewed enthusiasm, celebrating her curves and highlighting her ample cleavage in her costumes.

Melissa's physical transformation progressed, and her prowess in horror cosplay flourished. With her pale white skin and flaming red hair, she found herself subject to a surge in online attention and commentary regarding her appearance. However, rather than dampening her spirits, these remarks served to bolster her confidence significantly.

By the time 2014 unfolded, Melissa's life had undergone a significant transformation. She had embraced her newfound body, entered into her first serious romantic relationship with her boyfriend, and cultivated a steadily growing social circle.

At parties hosted by her new friends, Melissa encountered a woman who worked in online adult entertainment as a cam girl. This woman suggested to Melissa that she could make a substantial income by combining her passion for cosplay with online stripping.

With this chance meeting, Melissa was introduced to the world of online adult entertainment and the lucrative opportunities it presented. While she was accustomed to attention from cosplay, the prospect of becoming a cam girl introduced her to a whole new dimension of public scrutiny and financial potential.

Without hesitation, Melissa embraced the idea and embarked on her journey into the world of online adult entertainment. Before long, she quit her two part-time jobs to fully commit to her new role as a cam girl. Adopting the name "Two Thorned Rose" in the digital realm, Melissa's online persona rapidly gained popularity. Things were finally starting to happen for Melissa Turner.

As Melissa's success as a cam girl soared, she recognized the potential for even greater financial gains by transitioning from stripping to performing full-fledged porn scenes. Boldly asserting her prowess, she boasted of her exceptional oral sex skills in her online persona and brought these claims to life in explicit performances.

Maintaining her signature blend of cosplay and horror elements, Melissa's videos continued to captivate audiences with their unique flair. In 2016, Melissa and her boyfriend embarked on a collaborative venture in which they established a small studio catering to fellow cam models. Their studio quickly gained traction within the adult entertainment community by offering rental space and equipment.

However, as the demands of their business venture intensified, strains began to emerge in the relationship between Melissa and her boyfriend. Eventually, the pressures proved too much to bear, leading to their mutual decision to part ways. Despite the dissolution of their romance, Melissa remained steadfast in her pursuit of success within the industry.

During the summer of 2017, while recuperating from two surgeries to tighten her skin after her extreme weight loss, Melissa matched with Matt Tressler on the dating app Tinder. The two quickly fell in love and moved in together.

———

Matt Tressler, originally from Hopkinton, Massachusetts, a small town with a population of 18,000, was known for his fun-loving nature and strong work ethic. He shared a close bond with his family and had a deep love for animals, particularly cats and dogs.

After completing his studies at Westfield State University, Matt secured a position as a general manager at a local

Italian restaurant. However, his struggles with substance abuse issues prompted him to consider a significant life change.

In 2015, Matt made the decision to move to Tampa, Florida, to be closer to his brother, Sean. Sean recognized that Matt needed a fresh start and supported his relocation, hoping that the distance from his past struggles and the prospect of a job in the construction industry would provide him with new opportunities and a path toward a more stable, fulfilling life.

———

By Christmas of 2018, Matt and Melissa found themselves in an exciting chapter of their lives. Their relationship had blossomed over time, and both enjoyed relative success in their careers. Matt was okay with Melissa's career and even appeared in some of her videos.

In 2019, Matt and Melissa achieved a significant milestone in their lives by purchasing a home together. The couple bought a spacious four-bedroom, two-and-a-half-bathroom house located on White Barn Way in Riverview, Florida. This accomplishment was particularly impressive considering their relatively young age.

Their new home, situated in the desirable community of Boyette Farms, boasted ample space and a pool in the backyard. Accompanying their home were four cats and an adorable puppy named Lanta.

On January 11, 2019, as Matt celebrated his 25th birthday, he took to Facebook to express his gratitude for the numerous blessings in his life, reflecting on the positive developments in his relationship, career, and personal growth.

On their social media profiles, both Melissa and Matt portrayed themselves as the picture-perfect couple. As with many who document their lives on social media, however, life isn't always as it seems.

Despite the happy image Melissa and Matt portrayed on social media, their relationship faced a significant challenge when Melissa's former boyfriend allegedly became jealous of her new relationship with Matt. According to reports, he went so far as to threaten Matt with a gun, creating a tense and potentially dangerous situation for the couple.

However, in the aftermath of the ordeal, Melissa and Matt made a conscious effort to maintain the appearance of a happy and stable relationship on their social media platforms. They continued to share posts and pictures that depicted them as a loving, carefree couple, seemingly unaffected by the recent threat.

Behind closed doors, however, Matt and Melissa's relationship was falling apart. The couple frequently engaged in heated arguments, and Matt's drinking habit escalated, causing him to gradually withdraw from his friends and family.

Matt's brother, Sean, watched the deterioration of his brother's relationship with Melissa, recognizing the increasingly toxic nature of their interactions. Sean grew concerned as he witnessed the negative impact the relationship was having on Matt's well-being and personal life.

The couple's neighbors also became aware of the strain in Matt and Melissa's relationship, often overhearing the couple as they shouted at each other.

By that September, friends had noticed that Matt's posts

about their seemingly wonderful relationship had tapered off. It was clear his mindset had shifted.

———

On October 18, 2019, emergency services received a frantic 911 call from Melissa Turner at 8:45 a.m. Melissa frantically told the operator that Matt was unresponsive in the backyard of their home, and she had no idea what had happened.

Police and emergency medical responders arrived at the home adorned with Halloween decorations to find Matt Tressler on the back patio near the pool. Despite their efforts to administer CPR, it was clear that Matt had died hours earlier, as rigor mortis had already set in. He was pronounced dead at the scene.

Matt's body bore signs of a brutal attack, with punctures and lacerations scattered across him. Defensive wounds were evident on his forearms, while a deep stab wound was discovered in the center of his back. A tactical knife was found at the scene covered in blood.

When investigators questioned Melissa Turner at the Hillsboro County Sheriff's office, she was covered in blood and wearing latex gloves given to her by an officer. Melissa claimed the day leading up to his death was like any other day. They had been drinking throughout the day, but by 11:00 p.m., she was tired and fell asleep on a chair in her office.

When she woke up in the same chair just after 8:00 the next morning, she was confused because the kitchen was covered in blood. She told investigators that she rushed upstairs to see if Matt was in their bed, but when she found he wasn't, she started looking for him throughout the house. That was when she found him on the back patio and began administering CPR.

When questioned by investigators about any scratches or cuts, Melissa initially denied having any. However, when prompted to remove her latex gloves, she appeared surprised to find a deep cut spanning the entire palm of her right hand.

When investigators asked how she got the two-and-a-half-inch gash, she said she hadn't even noticed it was there. This claim, however, contradicted her earlier statement, as she had already mentioned it to the 911 operator during her call.

Melissa then said she thought she had cut herself when picking up broken glass in the kitchen, but it was obvious to investigators what had happened. They believed her hand, covered in blood, had slid down the length of the tactical switchblade as she was stabbing Matt.

During the interrogation, investigators asked if there had been any arguments the evening before, but she insisted they hadn't argued and neither of them was ever violent. It was becoming clear that Melissa couldn't keep her stories straight. Just hours earlier, she had told first responders at the scene that she and Matt had been arguing the night before.

Melissa Turner then admitted to detectives that there may have been some arguing, but she downplayed its significance, stating that it wasn't anything major and she couldn't even recall what it was about.

Until this point, Melissa had maintained that she didn't know how Matt had died. However, when investigators revealed that Matt's body had been discovered with stab wounds, she appeared taken aback. Melissa claimed to have no knowledge of him being stabbed and expressed confusion over how such an event could have occurred.

Investigators went door to door, speaking to Melissa and Matt's neighbors to see if they had seen or heard anything that night. What they learned blew apart Melissa's story of ignorance.

Across the street from their two-story home, a neighbor had installed a Nest security camera above their garage door. The camera pointed directly toward Melissa and Matt's house. Although the video didn't show any visual disturbances that night, the recorded audio told a very different story.

Between 4:00 a.m. and 4:45 a.m., the security camera captured audio of intense arguing. While Matt's voice couldn't be heard, Melissa's screams were chilling. Rather than expressing fear, they conveyed a sense of profound anger.

Among the sounds of shattering glass, Melissa screamed,

> "You stay!" "Dammit!" "Wake up!" "I hate you!" "Get up! Now!" "So, fucking die! Stay down!" "Get up! Wake up!" "I hate you! Go fuck yourself!" "Fuck you!" "Bitch, get up!"

Finally, at 4:44 a.m., her final screams were,

> "No!" "What have I done?"

Melissa claimed to have no memory of any events occurring at 4:00 a.m., but she quickly changed her story when detectives confronted her with the recorded evidence of the argument. Melissa then admitted that she had lied.

Melissa now told detectives that Matt had awakened her because he was still up drinking at 4:00 a.m., which upset her. She claimed that she had screamed at him to "stay down" because he was so drunk he couldn't stand up.

When detectives questioned Melissa about the cut on her palm, she once again altered her account of the events. According to her new story, Matt had been threatening to cut himself with the knife, which she claimed was a frequent occurrence. Melissa told detectives that she had sliced her palm while attempting to wrest the knife from him.

As the interrogation continued, detectives grew increasingly skeptical of Melissa's explanations, believing that she was desperately fabricating new justifications on the spot. Following an extensive interrogation lasting several hours, Melissa Turner was formally charged with second-degree murder that same evening.

Melissa was released on bail after her arrest and gave numerous interviews with television news shows, often crying in front of the cameras. Each time, her story continued to evolve.

Contrary to what she had told detectives at the time of her interview, Melissa now claimed that, after she had wrangled the knife from Matt, he had wrapped his hands around her neck and started to strangle her. She told television cameras that this was when she had "lightly" stabbed him in the back to get him off of her.

Melissa alleged that Matt had then assaulted her, pushing her into the kitchen counter and causing a "pretty severe" head injury. From that moment onward, she claimed her memory had become fragmented, and she eventually found herself back in her office, where she lost consciousness. She portrayed herself as the true victim, asserting that she had endured abuse at the hands of Matt.

Emergency medical staff, however, had no record of Melissa complaining of or being treated for a head injury of any kind on that night. Additionally, she had said to detectives during questioning that Matt had never been violent in any manner; it was only in the weeks before her trial that Melissa made any claims of abuse.

———

Investigators discovered that the couple had an ADT security camera installed inside their home. After reviewing the footage from the night of the murder, they saw Matt calmly and slowly walking through the house, appearing composed and collected. In stark contrast, the video captured Melissa frantically running back and forth, displaying signs of intense anger and agitation.

At 4:01, the ADT camera showed Melissa running from the kitchen with her arms flailing, clearly upset. Seven minutes later, she stood facing the front door in a daze, seemingly talking to herself. The video showed her right hand covered in blood. Moments later, she walked back into the kitchen.

———

During her 2022 trial, Melissa Turner took the stand in her own defense. As part of her emotional display, which some observers found to be forced, she cried and maintained that Matt had been abusive toward her. She claimed he would frequently push her against walls, punch holes in the walls with his fists, and inflict injuries on himself through cutting, burning, and stabbing.

She insisted Matt often stared off into the corner of the room with a crazed look, telling her a demon was standing there. She claimed he would often talk in a different voice, as if he were possessed. According to Melissa, Matt would say things like, "What's the matter, little girl? Are you scared? Because Matt's not here anymore," in this altered state.

During the trial, the prosecution challenged Melissa about the memories she claimed had suddenly resurfaced three years after her initial questioning by detectives. Melissa attributed her previous lack of recollection to a head injury she allegedly sustained. However, a crime scene technician who had examined Melissa on the day of the murder provided testimony contradicting her claim, stating that she exhibited no signs or evidence of a head injury at that time.

Prosecutors presented compelling evidence from the ADT home security camera footage, which depicted Melissa walking back into the kitchen with her hand already covered in blood. This crucial detail suggested that Matt had likely been stabbed and was bleeding out on the kitchen floor at that point. Notably, the timestamp on the ADT video coincided with the timestamp from the audio recordings captured by the neighbors across the street, further corroborating the sequence of events.

Although the judge had forbidden the prosecution from mentioning that Melissa made her living acting out explicit scenarios online as a cam model, the prosecutor boldly accused Melissa of faking her tears on the stand as she described the night she attacked Matt.

> "You're crying right now. Is that what's happening? Are you crying right now? Or are you crying right now because you can just cry on cue?"

As Melissa replied, her tears seemed less and less genuine. Her emotions appeared inconsistent and exaggerated throughout her testimony, suggesting a tendency toward dramatic behavior, as portrayed by the prosecution.

The defense contended that Melissa had been subjected to ongoing abuse from Matt and asserted that she had acted in self-defense by stabbing him once in the back. They argued that any other injuries on his body, including the fatal slice on his arm, were self-inflicted.

Additionally, the defense introduced an expert witness who suggested that the prosecution had manipulated the audio captured by the Nest security camera. They alleged that Melissa's voice had been amplified while Matt's voice had been suppressed, creating a misleading impression of the altercation.

The prosecution, on the other hand, presented evidence that pointed to a struggle and Matt's desperate attempt to escape the house after being stabbed. They highlighted the fact that, despite bleeding profusely on the kitchen floor, Matt had made a significant effort to remove a window screen and flee to the pool area outside.

The prosecution argued that this behavior was inconsistent with the scenario of self-inflicted wounds, as they questioned why Matt would go to such lengths to leave the house if he had indeed stabbed himself. They asserted that Matt's actions clearly indicated he was trying to get away from a threat inside the house, casting serious doubt on Melissa's account of the events from that night.

Data from Matt's smartwatch revealed that his heart had stopped beating at 5:11 a.m. However, Melissa did not contact 911 until 8:45 a.m., several hours later.

Ultimately, the jury didn't believe Melissa Turner's tears were genuine. One jury member later told reporters that once he heard her scream "What did I do?" on the audio recording, any doubt that he had of her innocence was gone.

On February 18, 2022, she was convicted of second-degree murder. One month later, Melissa Turner was sentenced to twenty years and six months in prison. She will be eligible for release before her fiftieth birthday.

CHAPTER 4
ROOM 308

On October 26, 2018, Grace Millane left her home in Essex, England and drove to Heathrow Airport. The adventurous and outgoing twenty-one-year-old had recently graduated from the University of Lincoln with a bachelor's degree in advertising and marketing, but before settling into the working world, she planned a gap year to backpack around the world.

Grace, born to parents David and Jillian Millane, was the youngest sibling behind her two older brothers, Michael and Declan. Sociable, lively, and deeply family-oriented, she held a profound love for all things creative and artistic. Known for her kindness, she selflessly donated her long hair to the charity Little Princess Trust, ensuring it would be made into wigs for children with cancer, reflecting her caring nature.

Grace arrived in Peru, eagerly anticipating her upcoming adventure and ready for the next phase of her life. She spent three weeks in Peru and then visited several places in South America before flying to Auckland, New Zealand on November 30.

Grace arrived in Auckland, New Zealand and checked into the Base Backpackers hostel located in the city center. There, she met the other travelers who would be her roommates during her stay.

After checking into her hostel, Grace spent her first day in Auckland sightseeing around the city. She shared updates about her trip on social media, texting photos to friends and family back home. In her downtime, Grace also used the popular dating app Tinder to look for potential matches in the area.

After swiping right on Jesse's profile earlier that day, Grace chatted with him for hours. His profile displayed a picture of Jesse dressed in a black shirt and gray tie, and his bio said he worked as a manager in the oil industry. At first, Grace seemed hesitant about the meetup, but after further conversation, she finally agreed to meet her date and grab drinks together.

On Saturday, December 1, around 5:30 p.m., Grace left the hostel and headed into the city center. She was dressed up for a date, wearing a black knee-length dress paired with white shoes and carrying a small purse.

Grace walked five short minutes to Sky City, a bustling entertainment complex in the heart of the city. The multi-level mall boasted a casino, three luxury hotels, numerous popular bars and restaurants, and the iconic Sky Tower. Standing at 1,076 feet tall, the tower housed an observation deck offering panoramic views of Auckland.

Grace and Jesse met in the light rain outside of Sky City and walked to Andy's Burgers & Bar, a lively hamburger restaurant. The two sat at the bar, ordered drinks, and got to know one another.

After almost an hour of drinks and chit-chat, Grace and Jesse were clearly hitting it off, so they left Sky City and decided to bar-hop. They walked around the corner to the Mexican Cafe, where they shared two large jugs of margarita and a sangria, then later continued on to The Blue Stone Room a few blocks away for several more drinks.

In the span of four hours, the two had consumed twenty-five drinks. Grace and Jesse were both tipsy and had shared their first kiss while sitting at a corner table of the bar. When Jesse got up to use the restroom, Grace sent a quick text to her friend Ameena back in England to let her know how the date was going.

> "I click with him so well. We're getting smashed together and just having a great night. I will let you know what happens tomorrow."

However, when Grace got up to use the restroom, Jesse spent those quick minutes snooping through Grace's purse.

Just before 10:00 p.m., Grace and Jesse left the bar arm-in-arm.

———

The next day, Sunday, December 2, was Grace's twenty-second birthday. Her friends and family back home bombarded her phone with birthday wishes, and more friends posted birthday greetings on her Facebook page. However, they quickly became worried when Grace didn't respond to any of her messages.

Grace had been traveling with two mobile phones as a precaution in case one was misplaced or malfunctioned.

However, all calls to both of her phones were now going straight to voicemail, indicating they were either turned off or had dead batteries. This was highly unusual, as Grace typically shared daily photos and updates from her trip without fail. The lack of communication from her that day caused growing concern among her friends and family.

On December 5, after three days without contact from his daughter, David Millane called the Auckland Police to report Grace missing.

Auckland Police contacted the Base Backpackers hostel where Grace had been staying. Staff confirmed that she hadn't returned to her room on the night of December 1 after her Tinder date. At first, authorities didn't suspect foul play, since Grace's possessions were still at the hostel. One theory was that she may have stayed with some new acquaintances and neglected to update her family and friends. However, Grace's parents insisted that would be completely out of character for their daughter, who was usually very communicative and responsible about keeping in touch, especially when traveling alone in a foreign country.

Detectives investigating Grace's disappearance benefited from a significant amount of CCTV camera footage captured throughout Auckland's city center. This comprehensive surveillance network allowed them to efficiently retrace Grace's path on the evening of her disappearance. By carefully reviewing the footage from multiple locations, investigators were able to chronologically map out her movements that night. The video evidence also led them to quickly identify the man she had met.

On the very night Grace was last seen, she changed her profile picture on Facebook. A comment was posted beneath the picture, reading, "Beautiful. Very radiant." The person who left this comment was identified as the very same man Grace had been on a Tinder date with that evening—her last known contact before she vanished.

Investigators identified the man as Jesse Kempson, who at the time was staying in Room 308 at the CityLife Hotel, located directly across the street from the bar where he and Grace were last seen together.

A month earlier, Kempson had written a long post on his Facebook profile apologizing for his bad decisions, arrogance, and selfishness:

> "Hey everyone I just wanted to touch base with you all. I've made a lot of bad decisions in my life so far that I'm not proud of some of which have greatly affected others. I firstly want to extend the most sincere apologies for this.
>
> I've done a lot of reflection over time and have narrowed down the cause of it all and with that being said I believe you all deserve to know. My clear arrogance and selfishness has truly affected the relationship I have with people in my personal life.
>
> I know that I was growing up, emotionally, mentally. When we grow up, we make mistakes. That's how we improve! In the exam of life, you can't retest yourself with the same question paper! But with that being said we can change

how we treat each other and over time I've learnt that every action has a reaction but I've also learnt how much compassion we all have as people I've recently been diagnosed with severe anxiety and currently take medication to keep this under control.

Putting all that aside I just want anyone who I've hurt/let down to know I'm truely sorry from the bottom of my heart."

Twenty-six-year-old Jesse Kempson's childhood was marked by frequent relocations following his parents' separation. Raised partially by his grandparents, he grew distant from much of his family. People who were acquainted with him, however, consistently described Jesse as a pathological liar.

Jesse Kempson's penchant for deception knew no bounds, and he spun elaborate lies ranging from claims he was the cousin of a popular professional rugby player to falsely professing to be terminally ill with cancer. His web of deception ensnared employers, landlords, partners, and even his own family and friends.

Jesse's compulsive lies unraveled repeatedly, resulting in frequent evictions from his apartments and job terminations. One former landlord recounted how Jesse claimed he was a professional softball player recruited by New Zealand's national team, the Black Sox. However, after eight weeks of excuses for not paying rent, the landlord contacted the Black Sox management, again exposing Jesse's lies.

At the CityLife Hotel, Jesse claimed to hold a high-ranking managerial position at Woolworths, while in reality, his rent was being paid by state benefits. His most recent job in telephone sales ended with his firing on December 1—the same day he crossed paths with Grace Millane.

Jesse Kempson, the last person known to have been with Grace on the night she vanished, became a central focus of the police investigation. Authorities called Jesse in for questioning, hoping to gather crucial information to help find the missing girl.

———

When Jesse Kempson was questioned on December 5 about his date with Grace Millane, he told detectives that all-in-all the night had been a success. He said he initially wanted to meet with her in a busy public area because he was concerned for his own safety—he said wasn't sure if she was real, since he had only spoken to her through Tinder messages.

He explained that they went to several bars and had a wonderful time together. He claimed, as they had left the Blue Stone Room at the end of the evening, he walked toward his apartment while she walked in the other direction, toward her hostel. According to Jesse, that was the last time he had seen her.

Jesse said the two of them had plans to get together the following day, but when he woke up and tried to message her, she had unfriended him on Tinder, and he was unable to contact her.

When detectives asked for a voluntary DNA sample, Kempson quickly agreed, asserting he had nothing to hide.

Right away, detectives didn't buy his story and had a strong suspicion that Grace Millane was already dead. At the end of the interview, the lead detective made sure Kempson knew he was the primary suspect in the disappearance and possible murder of Grace, but without definitive evidence, he was released.

———

Investigators pored through six terabytes of security camera footage from all over the city, trying to piece together what had really happened that night between Jesse Kempson and Grace Millane. What they discovered was horribly disturbing.

CCTV footage from the three bars verified that the couple had drunk a large amount of alcohol that night as they bar-hopped through the city. Cameras picked up their first kiss at the Blue Stone Room, and Jesse strangely looking through her purse as she went to the restroom. But as they left the restaurant, they hadn't parted ways as Jesse had told detectives. Cameras showed they both crossed the street arm-in-arm and stumbled into the CityLife Hotel, where Kempson rented a room. Cameras followed as the elevator stopped on the third floor, and the two walked off—but from that point on, Grace Millane was never seen leaving the building.

The morning after, on Grace's twenty-second birthday, Jesse Kempson entered the elevator alone at 8:00 a.m. and left the hotel. Additional security cameras picked him up five minutes away at The Warehouse, a nearby shopping center, where he purchased a large suitcase and cleaning supplies before returning to his apartment.

Just before noon, he left the hotel again and took a taxi to a car rental location, where he rented a red Toyota Corolla. CCTV cameras recorded his every move.

Several hours later, Jesse met with another woman he had connected with on Tinder. She later disclosed that the conversation had turned disturbing, discussing topics such as burying bodies and eluding the police. Feeling deeply unsettled by his remarks, she declined Jesse's offer to ride in his car and opted to make her own way home.

Just after 8:00 p.m., cameras captured Kempson renting a Rug Doctor carpet cleaning machine. As he wheeled the machine to his rented hotel room, he explained to the hotel staff that he had spilled some wine on the carpet and needed to clean it.

At 9:30 that evening, hotel cameras recorded Kempson wheeling two large suitcases out of the building, where he then placed them in the rented Toyota.

On the morning of December 3, Kempson was up early. Just before 7:00 a.m., he drove to a hardware store where he purchased a red shovel. Security cameras then lost sight of him until he returned to his apartment almost three hours later.

The remainder of the day, Kempson dropped off items at a dry cleaner and power washed the Toyota Corolla before returning it. Each move was recorded by CCTV cameras throughout the city.

On December 5, Kempson left his apartment with a heavy duffle bag slung over his shoulder. He walked to various locations throughout the city, dropping items from the bag into public trash cans.

When Jesse returned to the hotel and saw police officers at the front desk, he quickly turned around and walked hastily down the street. The officers chased after him, though, and brought him in for questioning.

After investigators viewed the security footage of Kempson's movements in the days after Grace's disappearance, he was brought in for a second line of questioning.

When confronted with the enormous amount of CCTV footage tracking his every move, Kempson changed his story. This time, he claimed he had accidentally strangled Grace Millane during violent but consensual sex.

Kempson said Grace had mentioned that she had enjoyed the movie *Fifty Shades of Grey* and asked if they could involve bondage in their sex. He claimed that they were having sex and ended up on the floor when she asked him to put his hands around her throat.

Afterward, Kempson claimed he then fell asleep in the shower, and he didn't realize that Grace had died until he woke up the next morning and found her still lying on the floor. He insisted her death was an accident. Kempson said he then panicked, put her body in a suitcase, and drove out of town to bury her.

Jesse Kempson led investigators to a remote location in the Waitakere Ranges National Park, where he had buried Grace Millane's body in a suitcase just ten yards from the road.

Forensic pathologists determined Grace Millane had died from manual strangulation at the hands of Jesse Kempson. The weight of his considerable force had caused blood vessels to burst in her face and left eye, and her nose had bled profusely. Severe bruises were found on her upper arms, neck, and shoulders. Medical experts believed the attack lasted between five and ten minutes and required constant, unrelenting pressure.

———

Upon searching Jesse Kempson's hotel room, the forensic team discovered that the floor was still extensively stained with blood, even though Kempson had made efforts to clean and conceal the evidence of his crime.

The forensic examination of Jesse Kempson's computer revealed a disturbing array of searches conducted on December 2, which served as compelling evidence of his guilt. His search history included terms related to the decomposition of human remains, such as "rigor mortis," and inquiries about scavenging birds like vultures in New Zealand. Furthermore, he had researched practical means to conceal the crime, searching for "duffel bags with wheels," "industrial-strength carpet cleaners," "car hire," and "beaches close to Auckland."

Kempson had lied about falling asleep in the shower. In the hours immediately after her death, Jesse Kempson had spent the rest of the night viewing pornography on the internet and taking intimate photos of Grace's dead body.

———

The nation collectively mourned Grace's loss, with thousands paying tribute to her and participating in vigils. New Zealand Prime Minister Jacinda Ardern publicly extended her apologies to Grace's parents and pledged her own and the country's unwavering support, saying:

> "Your daughter should have been safe here, and she wasn't, and for that, I am sorry."

When the trial began a year later, in November 2019, Jesse Kempson still maintained that the death of Grace Millane resulted from consensual sex gone wrong. His defense argued that Jesse had panicked and attempted to hide her body after accidentally taking her life.

The prosecution presented a strong case against Jesse Kempson, bolstered by a substantial body of evidence and numerous witness testimonies. They argued that Kempson's actions following Grace Millane's death were not driven by panic or the result of a tragic accident, but rather were calculated and deliberate. The prosecution asserted that Kempson had meticulously and callously attempted to hide his crime, weaving an intricate tapestry of lies and deception to conceal the truth. They pointed to his systematic efforts to clean the crime scene, dispose of evidence, and construct a false narrative as clear indications of his guilt and the premeditated nature of his actions.

The prosecution made a chilling assertion in their case against Jesse Kempson. They contended that Kempson had relentlessly maintained intense pressure on Grace Millane's neck for an extended period, lasting between five and ten minutes. This duration, they argued, far exceeded the time it would have taken for Grace to lose consciousness and become unresponsive. The prosecution emphasized the disturbing reality that Kempson had continued to strangle

Grace long after she had gone limp and lifeless, leaving no doubt about the deliberate and fatal nature of his actions.

To further build their case, the prosecution called upon three women who had previously encountered Jesse Kempson through Tinder. These witnesses provided crucial testimony that shed light on Kempson's disturbing sexual proclivities. Each one recounted their intimate experiences, revealing that Kempson derived pleasure from engaging in masochistic and violent sexual acts, which often involved elements of bondage and choking.

Despite Jesse Kempson's claims of innocence, on December 22, 2019, he was found guilty of the murder of Grace Millane after only five hours of jury deliberation. Kempson received a sentence of life in prison with eligibility for parole in seventeen years.

The case sparked widespread outrage over how Grace's life was portrayed during the trial and how her killer rationalized her death. Many criticized what they saw as shameful and grotesque victim-blaming rather than placing responsibility squarely on the murderer himself.

Jesse Kempson's own family members provided damning characterizations of his personality and behavior. They described him as a pitiful fantasist prone to spinning elaborate lies. Kempson's step-brother offered particularly incriminating insights, revealing that Jesse had a long-standing habit of deceiving others about even the most trivial matters. He would weave complex webs of lies until he found himself trapped in a corner, unable to maintain his deceptions any longer. At that point, when confronted with the truth, Kempson would invariably break down emotionally, crying and fleeing the scene.

The following year, Jesse Kempson faced two additional trials, both conducted without a jury present and presided over by a judge alone. Two women had come forward after seeing Kempson in the media following his arrest for Grace's murder.

During the first trial in October 2020, an ex-partner detailed the physical, sexual, emotional, and financial abuse she endured while in a relationship with him. She recounted instances of Kempson holding knives to her throat, choking her, coercing her into sexual acts, and draining her bank account of ten thousand dollars. Kempson was found guilty on eight charges and sentenced to seven and a half additional years in prison.

In November 2020, Kempson faced yet another trial, this time for raping a young British tourist he had met on Tinder eight months before the murder of Grace Millane. He had coerced her, threatening her with violence not only against her but also targeting her family if she didn't comply. Kempson was found guilty and received an additional three and a half years in prison.

This brought the total of additional years to eleven, which would be served concurrently with his sentence for Grace's murder. When the judge delivered the guilty verdict for the rape, Jesse erupted in an aggressive rage.

"You are so full of shit, mate! You have no reason to convict me. You're full of shit."

On December 18, 2020, the Court of Appeals rejected his appeal, and it was reported that taxpayers had spent over NZ$400,000 on his legal aid. On June 29, 2021, the Supreme Court denied his final appeal, bringing an end to his legal efforts to reverse his conviction.

CHAPTER 5
THE CAPE CORAL MONSTER

On a warm afternoon in early May 1990, thirty-nine-year-old Jan Cornell and her eleven-year-old daughter Robin spent the day helping Jan's coworker, Lisa Story, move into the spare upstairs bedroom of their townhouse in Cape Coral, Florida.

The three-bedroom townhouse at the Courtyards of Cape Coral Condominiums was just three blocks from the Cape Coral Hospital, where both women worked—Jan as a lab technician for outpatient services and Lisa as a secretary.

Robin Cornell was a happy fifth grader who attended Tropic Isle Elementary, where she had recently become a safety patrol guard. Robin was known as a prankster who loved playing harmless tricks on her friends. She got good grades in school and loved animals and watching scary movies.

Several friends were in and out of the condo throughout the day to help move Lisa's belongings, and by the evening, they were finally finished. Jan, however, hadn't seen her boyfriend, Donnie, all day; she asked Lisa if she would watch Robin for the rest of the night while she went to his house to watch their favorite late-night television show.

At 10:30 that night, Jan set out her ironing board, knowing she would need to iron her work uniform early the next morning, as she had to be at work by 4:30 a.m.

Before she left, Jan told Lisa to lock both of the front door locks. One of these locks was broken and couldn't be opened with a key from the outside, so she said she would knock when she came home at around midnight.

Jan and Donnie watched their show that night, but Jan woke up in a panic at 4:00 a.m. She hadn't expected to fall asleep on the couch. With only a half hour to get to work, Jan quickly grabbed her keys and rushed to her car. She needed to get home, iron her clothes, and get to work.

Jan parked in the quiet parking lot at her condo and rushed toward the front door of her townhouse, remembering that she had told Lisa to lock both locks. As expected, the door was locked. Jan knocked several times, but neither Lisa nor Robin opened the door.

Jan walked to the other side of the building, hoping that maybe the sliding glass window would be unlocked, but she was puzzled to find it was wide open. Her first thought was that Robin had possibly let the cat out and forgotten to close the door. However, when she entered the kitchen to find the light still on, Jan had a sinking feeling something was wrong.

For a brief moment, Jan thought she heard footsteps coming down the stairs, but when she walked into the living room, there was no one there. Instead, she found the room in disarray. The living room had been ransacked, cabinets had been emptied, and the contents had been thrown throughout the room. Three empty beer cans lay on the dining room table.

Then she noticed someone had removed four framed photos of her two daughters, Robin and Jennifer, from the mantle and laid them face-up on the ironing board. Something wasn't right.

Jan had an eerie feeling and knew something terrible had happened. She rushed up the stairs to her bedroom, where she found Robin lying at the foot of the bed. Her daughter's nightgown had been pulled up around her neck, and her panties had been torn from her body. Jan looked into her little girl's eyes, which seemed frozen in terror.

Jan's first instinct was to perform CPR on her daughter, but she knew she was gone when she felt that her skin was cold and hard. Despite knowing her daughter was long beyond help, she still tried CPR; it was futile. Robin was gone.

Overcome with terror, Jan frantically called 911, all the while shouting at the top of her lungs to Lisa across the hallway, demanding to know what had happened. From her vantage point, Jan could see Lisa motionless on the bed, unaware in those chaotic moments that her friend had also been killed.

―――

When police arrived at the scene at 4:10 a.m., they found eleven-year-old Robin Cornell's lifeless body posed in a sexual position with a sex toy on the floor next to her. She had been smothered to death with a pillow and sexually assaulted after death. When investigators moved her body, they found one of her recent school photos on the floor beneath her. The killer had gone through her backpack to find the photo and intentionally placed it beneath her.

Across the hall, police found thirty-two-year-old Lisa Story lying silent on her bed. She, too, had been asphyxiated with a pillow and sexually violated after death.

Sadly, the security officer who normally patrolled the condo complex at night had called in sick.

From the evidence found at the scene, investigators believed the killer had smothered them, looked at a pornographic magazine, and then had sex with their lifeless bodies.

Investigators believe the killer had spent several hours in the house after the murders. Evidence showed he drank three beers and took a shower after killing them. He also left behind a pair of white socks and a horseshoe-shaped keychain with an Etienne Aigner charm and four keys—two of which were to an unknown Toyota vehicle.

Using a Luma-Lite, investigators also found Type O blood, several fingerprints, and a single bit of blond hair, which they believed could have belonged to the killer. The most important piece of evidence, however, was DNA. The killer had left his semen on the sheets, pillows, and Robin's body. Although DNA evidence was still in its infancy at the time, the FBI was in the early stages of establishing its CODIS national DNA database.

The killer had also stolen several items. Lisa's driver's license, credit cards, and checkbook were missing, as well as a 1990 gold Seiko wristwatch that Lisa had just purchased for her boyfriend's upcoming birthday. Engraved on the back was, "To Randy, Happy Birthday, 5-11-90, All My Love, Lisa."

Seasoned police officers openly wept as they left the horrific scene later that morning.

Police immediately began questioning hundreds of people in the area, including every resident of the 140-unit apartment complex. They spoke to friends of Jan and Lisa and checked for possible traffic stops of a Toyota that night. Initially, they found nineteen potential suspects in the area, but despite reviewing hundreds of tips, they found nothing.

In the days after the deaths, Tropic Isles Elementary School hired eleven trained relief officers to counsel young students who were traumatized by the violent death of their classmate.

―――

Jan Cornell grew frustrated over the first year of the investigation. Not only had there been no word from investigators regarding the DNA and fingerprints found at the scene, but the lead detective, Dick Wiley, had spent his time focused on Jan rather than looking for the killer.

Detective Wiley was one of the first officers to arrive on the night of the murder and immediately suspected that Jan was hiding something. Wiley believed the killings were not the random acts of a sexual psychopath. Instead, he believed the killer had broken into the house to steal drugs. He suspected that either Jan Cornell was a drug dealer or, at the very least, she was aware of who the killer was. Wiley suspected that Jan knew the killer but was afraid to say anything for fear that she would become his next victim.

His accusations infuriated Jan Cornell, her family, and the family of Lisa Story. DNA and fingerprints had been submitted to the Florida Department of Law Enforcement Crime Labs immediately after the murders, but a year later, the families were still waiting for any reports at all.

Insisting the investigation was their highest priority and they were doing everything possible to solve the crime, police created a re-enactment of the crime and aired it on a local crime television show. The segment focused on reports of a suspicious-looking man wearing a red baseball hat who had been seen standing outside the condo complex for several nights before the killings. Despite the local attention, however, the re-enactment generated no results.

———

Jan's frustration with the Cape Coral detectives and the lack of progress on the case only grew. She worked on her own for answers. She knew the killer could be anywhere by now. He could be in another state or even another country. Still, Jan believed the killer had to have talked to someone about the murders. There had to be someone out there who had information about the crime.

Determined to bring her daughter's killer to justice, Jan reached out to national television shows for help. Every week for months, she sent letters to Unsolved Mysteries, The Oprah Winfrey Show, Geraldo, and America's Most Wanted. America's Most Wanted replied but said, due to its tight production schedule, they couldn't air a segment about the murders. Unsolved Mysteries also responded that they couldn't cover the story, while Oprah and Geraldo didn't reply at all. Undeterred, Jan continued pleading for them to cover the story.

———

Four years into the investigation, Detective Wiley was promoted, and Detective Charlie Garrett took over the case.

Determined not to let the case go cold, he put an end to the focus on Jan Cornell and worked diligently to follow the evidence left at the scene. Despite the fingerprints and DNA, years continued to pass, and they were still no closer to finding a suspect.

Over the years, the case passed through six detectives, four Cape Coral Police Chiefs, and countless local reporters. Jan married her boyfriend, Donnie, and Robin's elementary school built a pond in her honor.

After fifteen years, Jan started feeling as though she had failed to fulfill her promise to her daughter about finding her killer. She turned to watching true crime television shows, finding in them a glimmer of hope that, one day, the killer would be caught and brought to justice.

She played a lone videotape that she had of her daughter over and over just to see her and hear her voice. In a drawer in her bedroom, she kept Robin's old purse, occasionally opening it and smelling inside—the scent of Now and Later candy and "Electric Youth" perfume reminded her of Robin.

At the Cape Coral police office, an entire room was dedicated to housing over 2,000 documents and items pertaining to the case, all neatly organized in plastic crates.

Cape Coral Police Department interviewed more than a dozen former detectives to work full time on the case. Former Detective Wiley applied for the position but didn't meet the strict requirements for the job. Plus, he was still convinced Jan and Lisa had been dealing drugs and wanted to continue pursuing that angle. Years later, he would be forcibly retired early after being found guilty of conduct unbecoming of an officer due to allegations he had tried to pick up a prostitute.

Cape Coral Police instead hired former New York Detective Fidel Balan to work exclusively on the case. He was paid $1,000 per week on several recurring six-month contracts to try to find the killer of Robin and Lisa.

Twice a week, Jan placed fresh flowers on her daughter's gravestone, which read, "Roses are Red, Violets are Blue." She and Robin's sister, Jennifer, placed heartfelt personal notices in the local newspaper each year on the anniversary of her death and on Robin's birthday.

> "In Loving Memory of Robin Marie Cornell: Sixteen years have gone by, and not a day goes by without you in our thoughts. The day is coming when you will actually rest in peace. We miss you dearly! All our Love, Jeni & Mom."

> "Today is 17 years since an evil soul took you from us. Not a day goes by that you are forgotten. I can't see you, touch you, hear you, but you are always so alive in my heart. I sometimes close my eyes and see your big smile and cute freckles across your nose. I remember your happy laugh and all your silly pranks. I miss you so much. I am keeping my promise to you, and justice will come. Never forgotten my little bird, I love you, Mom."

> "My sweet baby, today is a big day. You are 30 today, and I can still remember the day and minute you were born. You were so tiny, so beautiful, like a little bird. That's why we named you Robin. I can't be with you today, but someday we will hug again. I miss you so much

and cherish the 11 years I had you. We celebrate today for you, so my angel, Happy Birthday in Heaven. All Our Love, Mom and Jeni XOXO."

Finally, Jan received a glimmer of hope when America's Most Wanted agreed to broadcast the story of the murders. After sixteen long years, the case received the national attention Jan had tirelessly fought for. Over the next five years, the segment aired three times, generating a handful of leads each time. Unfortunately, despite these efforts, none of the leads ultimately led to the apprehension of the killer.

In 2016, twenty-six years after Robin Cornell and Lisa Story were murdered, Zachary Zieler was admitted for emergency surgery ten miles away in Fort Myers, Florida.

Zachary had been shot with a pellet gun by his father, fifty-four-year-old Joseph Zieler. Zachary's mother, Bonnie Kniceley, told police that after shooting his son, Zieler had fled.

Within a few hours, Joseph Zieler was discovered in a shed on his property, clutching a rifle. Zieler claimed to the police that he had acted in self-defense against his son, citing his son's larger stature. Nevertheless, he faced charges of aggravated battery—a felony offense in Florida.

In 2009, Florida passed a law requiring mandatory DNA collection from anyone charged with a felony.

Less than a month later, when Zieler's DNA was run through

the FBI's CODIS database, Cape Coral police announced that his DNA matched the DNA found on Robin Cornell's body.

Joseph Zieler would have been twenty-eight at the time of the murders of Robin Cornell and Lisa Story. Just two months after the double homicide, he was arrested for several other crimes, including dealing in stolen property, battery on a police officer, resisting arrest, and carrying a concealed firearm. It's unclear if any of the stolen property was from Jan Cornell's home. Zieler served only 135 days in jail for the crimes and managed to stay under the radar for the next twenty-six years.

When questioned about the killings, Zieler claimed he couldn't remember anything from his life before 1998 due to a bad motorcycle accident. He said he couldn't even remember his own parents' names or if he had ever lived in Cape Coral. He claimed that he was almost an invalid and his girlfriend, Bonnie, had needed to do everything for him ever since the accident.

Bonnie, however, told police that the excuse was nonsense. During his recorded phone calls with her, he explained to her how to get a bondsman, put the house up for collateral, sell off his possessions, and become his power of attorney. It was clear he knew how to take care of himself.

Also, just days earlier, after his arrest for shooting his son, he recalled where he was when his son was born in 1991. He also recalled how he had been living in Cape Coral when he met his girlfriend, Bonnie, twenty-six years earlier.

―――

After six years of delays, Joseph Zieler's double murder trial began in May 2023.

Florida State prosecutors were confident in their ability to secure a conviction. Given the violent nature of the case, the apparent premeditation, and the age of the victims, they pursued the death penalty.

Jan Cornell was the first to take the witness stand. She recalled the horrifying night when she found her daughter and roommate in her home. The jury was shown disturbing photos of Robin's nude and bloody body.

The prosecution built their case primarily on DNA evidence collected from Robin's body, as well as from a pillow and bedsheet found nearby. Genetic experts testified that the biological evidence unequivocally matched Zieler's DNA profile, with odds of one in 700 billion against it belonging to any other suspect.

The defense, however, focused their argument on implicating alternate suspects. Zieler's legal team emphasized crucial evidence: None of his fingerprints matched those found at the Cornell residence. Furthermore, blond hairs were discovered, while Zieler maintained that his hair had always been dark brown. They also asserted that Zieler was hundreds of miles away in Massachusetts at the time of the murders, although they failed to provide evidence to substantiate this claim.

Zieler's girlfriend, Bonnie, began dating him just one month before the 1990 slayings, and they remained together for the following twenty-six years. When Bonnie testified, she recounted Zieler's specific sexual fantasies, which eerily mirrored the position in which Robin's body had been found after her death. She further contradicted Zieler's assertions of memory loss, stating that in the twenty-six years they had been together, she had never observed any signs of memory issues in him.

Zieler took the stand to offer his own defense against the damning DNA testimony. Immediately after taking the stand, Zieler sat down and wiped his mouth, making sure to display his middle finger toward Jan and the prosecutors.

Initially, Zieler attempted to shift the blame for the murders onto his father or half-brother, suggesting that this could explain the DNA match. When this tactic failed, he claimed that his DNA was present at the scene because he had previously slept with Jan, insinuating that she had not changed her sheets.

However, during cross-examination, prosecutors challenged Zieler about a series of letters he had penned to Jan Cornell while he was incarcerated one year prior. These letters led to further charges of witness intimidation.

The content of the letters was shocking—Zieler claimed he had slept with Jan Cornell and her friend Leann Deller back in 1989, just six months before the murders. He then asserted that Jan was simply "too much of a pig" to wash the bedsheets, providing a justification for his DNA at the murder scene.

Zieler outlandishly stood by these fabrications, claiming it was the only plausible way his DNA had ended up in the apartment where two lives had mercilessly been stolen away.

The letters read,

> *IF YOU KNOWINGLY ALLOW THEM TO CONVICT THE WRONG MAN OUT OF SPITE AND VENGEANCE, I WILL DRAG THIS (AND YOU, ROBIN, AND LISA) THROUGH APPEALS ALL THE WAY TO THE US SUPREME COURT IN WASHINGTON, DC. I AM INNOCENT, I WILL PROVE IT, NO MATTER HOW LONG IT*

> **TAKES. DO YOU REALLY WANT THE REST OF YOUR LIFE TO BE SPENT IN COURT?**
>
> **THE <u>ONLY WAY</u> IS TO ADMIT YOU POSSIBLY COULD HAVE SLEPT WITH ME AS A NIGHT ENCOUNTER, AND YOU CAN'T REMEMBER.**

Zieler's defense attorneys told the jury that the presence of blond hair at the crime scene and the extreme violence of the act suggested a personal motive. It was not the act of someone who didn't know the victims.

On May 8, 2023, after several hours of deliberation, the jury returned a guilty verdict on all counts against Joseph Zieler. The jury voted by a ten to two margin to recommend the death penalty.

Five weeks later, on June 26, Zieler was brought into the courtroom to be sentenced. Zieler wore a bright-orange jumpsuit as he was led into the courtroom with his hands shackled to his waist. He bent his head slightly in a motion indicating that he wanted to whisper something in the ear of one of his attorneys, Kevin Shirley. However, when Shirley bent his head down next to his, in a lightning-fast move, Zieler swung his right elbow, covered in a spiderweb tattoo, and clubbed his lawyer squarely in the face.

Joseph Zieler was quickly wrestled to the ground by two officers. Shirley said, "I used to box. I've taken a lot better shots than that." He refused to press charges. Zieler later said he only wished he could have beaten his other lawyer, too.

Ten minutes later, with Zieler subdued and seated to hear his sentencing, he smiled for the courtroom cameras to reveal that he had written "KILLER" in black letters across the upper row of his false teeth. Minutes later, Joseph Zieler was sentenced to death.

The state later dropped harassment charges against him for the threatening letters sent to Jan Cornell.

CHAPTER 6
A BAD ACTOR

Orange County, California, stands out in the United States for its renowned beauty. With stunning beaches, luxury homes, and vibrant communities, it's widely regarded as one of the most desirable places to live in the nation.

Julie Kibuishi, a vivacious twenty-three-year-old student at Orange Coast College, called Orange County home. With a passion for dance and fashion design, Julie exuded warmth and charisma, effortlessly drawing people to her.

Among those captivated by her charm was Sam Herr, a twenty-six-year-old army veteran and former Private First Class in the U.S. Army 173rd Airborne who had served in Afghanistan.

Sam loved to travel and meticulously saved nearly every cent he made. By the time he left the military, he had saved $62,000 of his combat pay. He planned to pursue higher education and eventually re-enlist as an officer.

When Sam made his way back to Southern California, he decided to further his education by enrolling at Orange Coast College. It was there that he first encountered Julie, and as she began tutoring him in anthropology, their friendship quickly flourished. The nature of their relationship became a topic of speculation among their circle of friends, with some convinced that their connection had blossomed into a romantic one, while others maintained that they were simply close friends. Regardless of the varying opinions, one thing was clear: Sam and Julie shared an undeniable bond.

However, on the morning of May 22, 2010, Julie's mother grew increasingly worried when Julie failed to answer her phone. Concerned for her daughter's well-being, she reached out to Julie's friends for any information. Unfortunately, no one knew where Julie was, and their attempts to contact her also went unanswered.

Sam Herr's parents found themselves in a similar situation. Sam had made plans to spend the weekend with them, but as time passed, it became increasingly apparent that he would not be arriving as expected. Sam's phone uncharacteristically went straight to voicemail, leaving his parents worried.

Consumed by an ominous feeling of unease, Steve Herr, Sam's father, made his way to the Camden Martinique apartments where his son lived. Steve knocked several times, but he was met with an unsettling silence. The growing sense of dread that had been gnawing at him intensified, and Steve knew in his heart that something was amiss. Steve Herr reached for his key and unlocked the door to his son's apartment, bracing himself for what he might discover inside.

Everything in the apartment seemed to be in place until he reached Sam's bedroom. There, he made a horrific discovery: The lifeless body of a young woman lay half off the bed, a gunshot wound to the back of her head. Strangely, she was wearing a tiara. Her jean shorts had forcibly been cut from her body, and a chilling message, "All yours. Fuck you." was scrawled across the back of her sweater.

Sam's father wasted no time calling the police, but he was utterly clueless about the girl's identity. He had never seen her before, and even more troubling, Sam was nowhere to be found.

When police arrived at the scene, their attention was immediately drawn to the message scrawled in black marker across the woman's sweater. The content of the message, coupled with the circumstances surrounding the crime, led the officers to quickly identify the hallmarks of a domestic violence murder.

A purse lying on the floor nearby provided the victim's identity: It was Sam's friend, Julie Kibuishi. When detectives scrolled through the last text messages on her phone, it showed that Sam had sent her several messages the night before indicating that he was having some family issues and needed someone to talk to.

> Can you come over tonight at midnight alone? Going out for a bit. Very upset. Need to talk.

> I'm hurting with some family crap. Can't be alone.

> Please don't tell anyone. Please

> Please. No sex. I need to talk to someone. I'm really not doing well.

She replied,

> Yeah, that's fine, Sam. I'm here for you like family.

It appeared all but clear that Sam, who had extensive knowledge of firearms, had lured Julie Kibuishi to his apartment, where a sudden trigger caused him to sexually assault and murder his close friend. When investigators looked into Sam Herr's background, they were even more convinced that he had killed Julie in a fit of rage.

Eight years earlier, when Sam Herr was just eighteen, he was arrested along with fourteen other young men and charged with murder in connection to a gangland-style killing of a nineteen-year-old boy named Byron Benito.

Sam Herr and Byron Benito were close friends. On the night of the murder, Sam allegedly led his unsuspecting friend to an area behind a mobile home park, where Byron was attacked and killed by a group of suspected gang members. Sam Herr was one of the fifteen individuals arrested and charged with the murder.

The prosecution in that case believed that Sam played a role in luring Byron Benito to the location. Sam pleaded not guilty, and after going to trial in 2004, he was acquitted of the murder charges.

Despite his acquittal in the previous case, investigators were sure that Sam Herr had killed Julie Kibuishi. Sam's father, however, wasn't so convinced.

Sam Herr's father told detectives that his son had turned his life around and stopped associating with the group of friends he had been involved with in the past. His record from that point forward was spotless. He knew his son wasn't capable of cold-blooded murder.

Sam's family also said the text messages made no sense. The messages had mentioned family problems, but they weren't having problems at all. Sam and his parents were very close. Nevertheless, with Sam emerging as the primary suspect in Julie's murder, law enforcement agencies throughout southern California intensified their efforts to locate him.

Knowing Sam had money in the bank, investigators closely watched Sam's accounts for any activity. Sure enough, they discovered there had been two withdrawals of $400 each from an ATM in nearby Long Beach. However, when they watched the video taken from the teller machine, the person taking out money wasn't the muscular twenty-six-year-old they were expecting. Instead, it was a skinny teenager.

Later that day, there was activity on the debit card again. This time, a delivery pizza was ordered. Detectives acted swiftly, rushing to the pizza place to intercept the delivery before the driver departed. They managed to obtain the address and quickly dispatched a SWAT team to the location. However, upon arrival, instead of finding Sam Herr, they encountered a terrified sixteen-year-old named Wesley Freilich.

Wesley was completely perplexed by the officers at his door. He stepped aside and let them search the house. Officers expected to find Sam Herr hiding out in the house, but there was no sign of him.

Investigators questioned Wesley Freilich, who told them that he had indeed ordered the pizza and taken the money out of the ATM, but he said he was told to do so by a man named Daniel Wozniak. Wesley told detectives he had first met Daniel Wozniak while he was in middle school. Wozniak was an actor who was a friend of Wesley's mother, who worked as a drama teacher.

Wesley held twenty-six-year-old Daniel Wozniak in high regard, considering him a fun and trustworthy friend. So, when Wozniak approached him with a credit card under Sam Herr's name and requested a withdrawal, the naive teenager saw no reason to doubt him.

Daniel Wozniak had told Wesley he was working as a bail bondsman, and Sam Herr owed him money. The story seemed plausible enough to the impressionable boy, despite the lack of clarity on why he needed assistance from a seventeen year old.

Detectives soon learned that Daniel Wozniak was an unemployed community theatre actor who was engaged to a local actress, Rachel Buffett. Rachel had previously worked at Disneyland, playing Ariel from The Little Mermaid and Alice from Alice in Wonderland. Daniel and Rachel were performing together in the lead roles of a local production of the musical "Nine" and were scheduled to be married in two days.

Daniel Wozniak lived in the same apartment complex as Sam Herr, and when investigators looked further back at Julie

Kibuishi's text messages, they found that Sam had mentioned that he was going to help Wozniak with a project earlier that day.

Detectives very much wanted to speak to Daniel Wozniak. However, when they called his cell phone and asked him to come in to be interviewed, he declined. Wozniak explained that he was getting married in two days' time and was at his bachelor party.

Undeterred, detectives arrived at the Tsunami Sushi restaurant in Huntington Beach with an arrest warrant for Daniel Wozniak and took him into custody in the middle of his bachelor party.

Although investigators still believed Sam Herr had killed Julie Kibuishi, they knew that Wozniak was somehow involved.

As Wozniak tried to explain, police grew increasingly suspicious of him. When confronted with Wesley Freilich's story, Daniel Wozniak claimed that Sam Herr had roped him into a credit card fraud scheme.

According to Daniel, Sam had entrusted him with his ATM card, instructing him to gradually withdraw money from it. Sam's plan was to report the stolen card to his bank to recoup the losses.

In exchange for his participation, Daniel was promised a share of the funds, which he desperately needed due to his extensive mounting debts and imminent eviction, not to mention a wedding just days away and a honeymoon immediately afterward.

Wozniak vehemently denied any involvement in Julie's murder, insisting that he had no knowledge of the crime. He maintained that the last time he had seen Sam was at his apartment, just before Sam left with a man wearing a black hat. Sam and the man allegedly drove off together in a car, but he had no idea where they were going.

Detectives didn't buy his story for a minute. They knew Wozniak knew more and pressed him for answers. They could already book him as an accessory after the fact with the information he had given them thus far.

As the interrogation unfolded, Wozniak's behavior became increasingly erratic. Eventually, he admitted that his previous story involving the man in the black hat was a lie. Instead, Wozniak now claimed that Sam had visited him and revealed that he had killed his friend, Julie Kibuishi, while under the influence of alcohol and drugs.

According to Wozniak, Sam had been grappling with family problems and had invited Julie to his apartment. However, when Sam's sexual advances toward Julie were rebuffed, he grew angry and resorted to shooting her twice in the head in a fit of rage.

Daniel Wozniak claimed he had then driven Sam Herr to a local shopping center and hadn't seen him since.

Again, investigators weren't convinced. Daniel Wozniak's acting skills weren't as good as he thought they were. Detectives still didn't believe Wozniak was involved in the murder, but they were sure he knew more about Sam's location.

When asked for a DNA sample, Wozniak quickly complied, insisting he had nothing to hide. However, after investigators swabbed his cheeks and took his DNA, he became noticeably nervous, and his story changed even more.

Wozniak, worried that the police might find his DNA in Sam's apartment, told investigators about the different rooms of the apartment he had been in. Sensing that Wozniak was hiding something, the detectives confronted him and said they believed he was more involved in the case than he had admitted.

When asked if his DNA would be found on Julie Kibuishi, Wozniak insisted it wouldn't. He again said that he knew Sam had killed Julie but claimed he hadn't seen her body himself.

However, when the detectives informed him that he was being arrested as an accessory to murder, Wozniak's composure shattered, and he broke down.

> "I will talk to you about anything if it gets me to my wedding on Friday."

Wozniak then sat down with another detective and told yet another version of his story. He reluctantly admitted that he had seen Julie's body in Sam's apartment and saw two bullet wounds in her head.

There was a problem with his admission, however. There was no way Wozniak could have known that Julie had been shot twice just by looking at the massive wound on Julie's head. Detectives knew he had to have been present during the killing to know there were two shots.

When detectives bluffed and told Wozniak his DNA was found on Julie's body, he said he may have stood over her body. However, detectives pressed and told him that DNA doesn't just magically fall off—he had to have interacted with her. Wozniak still insisted he hadn't touched her.

Daniel Wozniak refused to talk further and returned to his jail cell, where he called his fiancée, Rachel Buffett. Rachel, however, had just spoken to Daniel's brother, Tim Wozniak. Police recorded the phone call:

> Rachel: "What did you do?"
>
> Daniel: "I helped Sam cover some stuff up and helped him get some drugs. That's it. I didn't murder anybody."
>
> Rachel: "My mom's working on canceling all the wedding plans now, and I just talked to Tim, and I need to make a phone call to the detective now."
>
> Daniel: "Why?"
>
> Rachel: "Tim says he has evidence with him. Or he knew where it was or something."
>
> Daniel: "Then I'm doomed."
>
> Rachel: "What?"
>
> Daniel: "Tim said that?"
>
> Rachel: "Yeah. Do you know that Tim has some evidence?"
>
> Daniel: "Yeah. Oh God, oh God, oh God."

Rachel: "Well, this is ridiculous and I have to go tell the detectives the truth."

Daniel: "No, don't. No, don't, don't, don't, don't. That can't be found."

Rachel: "No, babe, I'm gonna do it."

Daniel: "Listen to me. No, no. Trust me, please? I have to tell the truth on what I did. And I think you know what it is, and it's bad. Imagine the worst, and that's what I did."

After the phone call, Daniel Wozniak knew he was done. He asked to speak to detectives once again. This time, he finally wanted to come clean.

"I'm crazy, and I did it. I killed Julie, and I killed Sam. I killed them both. It was all just about the money. That's all."

Daniel Wozniak went on to explain how he had stolen a gun from his father's home and lured Sam to the attic at the Liberty Theatre on the Los Alamitos Joint Forces Training Base.

Wozniak had told Sam he needed help moving some boxes into the theatre. In the attic of the theatre, as Sam bent down to pick up a box, Daniel shot him in the back of the head.

Sam didn't die immediately and said, "Oh my gosh, I've been shot. I need help." Wozniak then shot him a second time, killing him.

Wozniak then used Sam's phone to send text messages to Julie Kibuishi, luring her to Sam's apartment. When she arrived, Wozniak was waiting inside and shot her twice in the back of the head. He then told detectives he staged the scene to make it appear she had been sexually assaulted. He partially removed her clothing, ripping and cutting her shorts, and wrote "All yours. Fuck you" on the back of her sweater in black marker.

Later that same evening, Wozniak went on to perform in a local production of the musical "Nine" alongside his fiancée, Rachel Buffett. The following morning, he returned to Sam Herr's apartment to carry out the gruesome task of dismembering Sam's body and disposing of the remains.

He cut off Herr's head, arms, and other body parts and disposed of them in the El Dorado Nature Center, a 105-acre nature preserve in Long Beach, California.

Wozniak packed the murder weapon, Sam's blood-stained clothing, and the tools used to dismember his body into a duffel bag. He then entrusted his brother, Tim, with the task of disposing of this incriminating evidence. However, Tim opted for a less discreet approach and merely tossed the bag over a fence.

Wozniak confessed that his sole motivation for the heinous murder of his two friends was financial gain. Struggling with more than $40,000 in debt, he was desperate to fund his extravagant wedding and planned honeymoon cruise with his fiancée. When Sam had casually mentioned his savings of over $60,000, Wozniak's first thought was to contemplate murdering his friend to steal the money.

Daniel Wozniak, confident in his acting abilities, believed he could deceive seasoned homicide investigators. However, he had overlooked a crucial detail: the impossibility of withdrawing $60,000 in $400 increments without raising suspicion.

Following his confession, Daniel Wozniak led detectives to the remains of Sam Herr. Police meticulously searched the park, ultimately recovering all of Sam's body parts except for one of his hands. In a cruel twist of fate, Sam's head was discovered on what would have been his 27th birthday.

Police also visited the residence of Daniel's brother, Tim, where they uncovered the duffel bag containing a wealth of incriminating evidence. This included the gun he had used to kill Sam and Julie, tools he had used to dismember Sam, Sam's passport and credit cards, and Sam's blood-covered clothing.

Tim Wozniak was subsequently arrested for his role as an accessory after the fact. Realizing the gravity of his situation, Tim quickly agreed to cooperate with authorities in exchange for a reduced sentence.

When investigators searched Daniel Wozniak's computer, they found he had searched "How to hide a body" and "Quick ways to kill someone."

The discovery of these incriminating searches on Wozniak's computer provided additional evidence of his guilt and helped establish his state of mind leading up to the murders. The searches demonstrated that the crimes were planned and deliberate rather than spontaneous acts of violence.

Despite the taped confession and substantial physical evidence against him, Daniel Wozniak pleaded not guilty and planned to argue during his trial that Rachel Buffett, his former fiancée, was the mastermind behind the murders.

While detectives and prosecutors didn't necessarily believe Rachel Buffett orchestrated the crimes, they suspected she knew more than she was admitting. She had also lied to detectives on multiple occasions during interviews.

Her initial support of Daniel's false claim about Sam being with a mysterious man in a black hat was particularly noteworthy: She had corroborated the story and told detectives she had seen the man herself.

A witness who was at the couple's apartment that day contradicted Rachel's story. He told detectives that both he and Rachel had seen Daniel and Sam leave together. Hours later, Daniel had returned alone, appearing visibly upset and distressed.

Given that the man in the black hat was later confirmed to be a lie, officers were understandably puzzled as to why Rachel Buffett had backed up this false narrative.

In 2012, Rachel was arrested and faced charges of being an accessory after the fact and obstruction of justice. Despite her public insistence of innocence, most notably during an appearance on the "Dr. Phil" show where Sam's father confronted her, she was eventually brought to trial in 2018. Rachel Buffett was convicted on two felony counts and received a sentence of thirty-two months in prison.

Daniel's brother, Tim, ultimately testified against him and entered a guilty plea for being an accessory after the fact. As part of his agreement with prosecutors, he received a sentence of four years of probation. However, Tim has encountered further legal issues since then.

―――

Daniel Wozniak's legal proceedings dragged on for longer than anticipated due to his attorney's use of various delay tactics. The defense filed multiple petitions claiming misconduct by both the arresting officers and the prosecution. Each of these petitions required arguments to be presented before a judge, which significantly slowed the progress of the case and extended the overall duration of the legal process.

This prolonged process frustrated the families of the victims and even the presiding judge. Daniel took advantage of the spotlight during this time, granting interviews from prison and appearing on television shows like "Lockup." This was much to the dismay of Sam and Julie's families, who felt the portrayal was overly sympathetic.

Finally, after a lengthy series of hearings and legal arguments that caused significant delays, Daniel Wozniak's murder trial began in 2016.

The prosecution presented a strong case against Daniel Wozniak, backed by compelling evidence that included witness testimonies, physical evidence, and, most significantly, Wozniak's own videotaped confession. In contrast, the defense put forth a weak argument, suggesting that Rachel Buffett was the true mastermind behind the murders and claiming misconduct on the part of the police.

The jury wasted no time in reaching a verdict. They deliberated for a mere hour before returning to the courtroom, unanimously finding Daniel Wozniak guilty of two counts of first-degree murder.

In the penalty phase of the trial, Daniel Wozniak's attempts to shift blame and the notable absence of character witnesses, even from his own parents, stood in sharp contrast to the outpouring of support for the victims, Sam Herr and Julie Kibuishi, from their loved ones. While friends and family members of Sam and Julie testified to the profound impact of their loss, Wozniak's defense presented a comparatively weak case for leniency. This glaring disparity in the support shown for the victims and the lack of compelling mitigating evidence on Wozniak's behalf likely played a significant role in the jury's quick decision to recommend the death penalty.

Following his sentencing, Daniel Wozniak sat on death row for three years. However, in May 2019, Governor Gavin Newsom issued an executive order that effectively placed a moratorium on all executions in the state. As a result, Wozniak's death sentence was put on hold, and he will instead serve the remainder of his life in prison without the possibility of parole.

The families of Julie Kibuishi and Sam Herr made their feelings about Governor Newsom's decision to halt executions in California clear. Despite the differing opinions on the death penalty itself, the victims' loved ones expressed their disappointment and frustration with the moratorium. They chose to voice their discontent publicly at a victim's rally held in Orange County, where they were joined by Matt Murphy, the lead prosecutor in the case, and other officials who supported their stance.

Regardless of the ongoing debate surrounding capital punishment, Daniel Wozniak's sentence ensures that he will spend the rest of his life imprisoned, never to experience freedom again.

CHAPTER 7
THE FRAME-UP

Pam Neumann was born in 1958 in Dellwood, Missouri, a suburb located north of St. Louis. Her father was employed at Union Electric, while her mother worked as a schoolteacher. Pam was the third child among four siblings and spent her upbringing in a well-organized, middle-class, Catholic household.

She attended River Garden High School, where she was a popular cheerleader. However, her life took a turn when she found herself pregnant before she graduated. Just three months before her senior prom, Pam married her high school sweetheart and had a daughter, Sarah.

Six years later, however, the couple divorced, and Pam quickly tied the knot once again—this time to Mark Hupp, who played minor-league baseball for the Texas Rangers. After giving birth to her son, Travis, the couple moved to Naples, Florida in 1989. However, when Pam's father passed away in 2001, the family of four moved back to Missouri to be closer to Pam's mother, and Mark took a job as a carpenter.

After their move to Missouri, Pam Hupp held clerical positions at various insurance companies and, for the most part, was known as a motivated worker, but she was fired twice when she was caught forging signatures.

During her time working for State Farm Insurance, Pam occasionally made cryptic comments suggesting she had ties to the FBI or another government agency. Her coworkers found these remarks both intriguing and perplexing. Pam would drop vague hints about having security clearance or past involvement with the FBI, but she always stopped short of providing any concrete details.

When pressed for more information, Pam would sidestep, saying she couldn't reveal anything further. Her colleagues weren't sure what to make of her claims. Some wondered if Pam might indeed have a shadowy background in government work, while others assumed she was simply telling tall tales to add an air of mystery to her otherwise ordinary life as an insurance clerk.

When Pam was accused of receiving insurance money for a roof that had never been replaced and forging her boss' signature, several employee vehicles in the State Farm parking lot were mysteriously vandalized by keying. Interestingly, a similar problem cropped up in Pam's quiet suburban neighborhood: The Hupps mostly kept to themselves, so neighbors found it peculiar when a rash of anonymous, menacing letters began circulating on their street. Some residents even had the disturbing experience of finding grisly piles of animal bones dumped in their yards.

In 2010, Pam Hupp stopped working and began claiming disability, citing back, neck, and leg pain. Later evidence revealed her ability to walk, run, and even attend Zumba classes without difficulty. Pam and Mark then began flipping houses to supplement the family's income.

Pam Hupp first met Betsy Faria in 2001 while working at the same State Farm Insurance office. Betsy, who worked as the office manager, was eleven years younger than Pam, but despite the age gap, they quickly bonded over their shared sense of humor and outgoing personalities.

Pam's pragmatic approach and adeptness in office dynamics earned her the role of being a mentor-like figure in Betsy's eyes. Betsy's warm nature and capacity to brighten any environment impressed Pam. Their workplace discussions spanned a spectrum of topics, from family matters to personal ambitions.

As the years passed and Pam left State Farm, the two drifted apart, yet they still considered each other the best of friends.

Everything changed, however, in January 2010, when Betsy received devastating news. She had been diagnosed with breast cancer. As she began the difficult journey of surgeries and chemotherapy treatments, Betsy found herself more in need of support than ever.

Pam, upon learning of Betsy's condition, reconnected with her immediately. She provided constant support, regularly checking in on Betsy and accompanying her to chemotherapy sessions. Feeling deeply touched by Pam's dedication, Betsy leaned on her friend during her darkest moments.

As Betsy's health declined, Pam assumed a caretaker role, managing her medical appointments, ensuring her well-being, and supporting Betsy's husband and teenage daughters.

In 2011, Betsy received the devastating news that the cancer had metastasized, spreading to her liver and kidneys. After pursuing every available treatment option, she was left with the grim reality that her condition was terminal. With heavy hearts, her doctors informed her that her remaining time was limited, forcing Betsy to confront the heartbreaking truth that her battle with cancer was nearing its end.

Devastated by the news, Betsy struggled with a profound sense of despair and hopelessness. She confided to her husband, Russ, that she'd prefer death over continuing to battle cancer. She believed it would alleviate stress for him and their daughters if she passed away rather than enduring further treatment.

Russ was concerned about his wife's mental health as Betsy began to withdraw into depression. She had tried slashing her wrists in the past. Despite the news, however, Betsy agreed to continue with the cancer treatments.

As Betsy grappled with her terminal illness, she was consumed by worry over her two daughters' financial futures. She had a $150,000 life insurance policy that named her husband as the beneficiary, but she feared he would squander the money if left to his own devices. At the same time, Betsy was hesitant to put the funds directly in her daughters' names, concerned they might not manage it wisely given their young age.

Faced with this dilemma and the urgency of her declining health, Betsy made a difficult decision. On December 22, 2011, Betsy changed the beneficiary on her life insurance policy to the one person she knew she could trust to set aside the money for her daughters—Pamela Hupp.

On December 27, after an understandably miserable Christmas, Betsy Faria awoke at her mother Janet's house, where she had spent the night. She had a chemotherapy treatment scheduled and planned to have her friend Bobbi, who used to babysit her as a child, accompany her to the appointment.

Betsy's husband Russ texted her at around noon, saying he would pick her up from her mother's place after the treatment. Pam, however, had her own plans. Pam showed up at Janet's house that morning, intending to drive Betsy to her chemo session, but she and Bobbi had already gone. Undeterred, Pam drove to the cancer center anyway.

Betsy was surprised to see Pam at the treatment center, as she had specifically asked Bobbi to take her so they could spend some one-on-one time together. Nonetheless, Pam stayed by Betsy's side throughout the remainder of her treatment.

Afterward, instead of letting Russ pick Betsy up as planned, Pam insisted on driving Betsy home herself. Just before 3:00 p.m., Betsy messaged her husband about the change in plans, letting him know that Pam would be bringing her home.

At 7:00 p.m., Pam dropped Betsy off at the house she shared with Russ. Russ was out for a weekly movie night with friends that evening, so Betsy expected to be home alone.

Minutes later, at 7:27, Pam called Betsy to let her know she had made it home safely, but the call went to voicemail.

Russ Faria spent the evening watching movies at the home of his friend Michael Corbin, alongside several other friends, as they did almost every Tuesday night. Just after 9:00, he stopped by Arby's Restaurant for a late-night snack before driving back home.

Russ walked into the home to find Betsy on the floor next to the couch. At first, he thought she was just sick from the chemo, but then he saw the blood. Her wrists had been slashed, and blood was spattered all over her body and pooled beneath her. Her throat had been slashed, and the handle of a kitchen knife was still sticking out of her neck.

Russ dialed 911 in a panic, his words barely coherent as he struggled to breathe. With Betsy's slashed wrists in sight and her recent discussions about not wanting to live echoing in his mind, he informed the operator that his wife had killed herself.

When emergency crews arrived, however, it was glaringly obvious that Betsy's death was not suicide. The blood Russ mistook for spatter from her wrists was actually from fifty-five stab wounds beneath her clothes. Her lungs, abdomen, spleen, and liver had all been punctured with the serrated kitchen knife that was stuck in a bone in her neck. She had been stabbed in her eye and several times in her skull. Her wrists weren't just slashed—they were cut to the bone. A second knife lay on the floor near her body.

Massive amounts of blood covered the carpet in the room. Although the blood that had pooled around her was still wet, the blood on her wrists and head had hardened. Her body was cold and had begun to stiffen. The medical examiner determined she had been dead for at least an hour, possibly longer.

When officers at the scene tried to calm Russ down, he seemed to go in and out of hysteria. They described him as "over the top." On the 911 call, he had been barely able to put together words, and the operator had needed to remind him to breathe. However, when an officer engaged him in casual conversation about their shared childhood neighborhood, Russ appeared to calm down. Russ even laughed, momentarily easing his distress—but the officer on the scene took that as suspicious.

A pair of Russ' slippers were found with blood on them, and he was brought into the police station for questioning. From the outset, detectives pinned the blame on Russ for his wife's murder, particularly because he had said that Betsy had killed herself. This seemed a ridiculous assumption considering the condition of her body. When given a polygraph, Russ failed.

During ten hours of interrogation, Russ insisted he had nothing to do with his wife's death and that he was with friends watching *Conan the Barbarian* for most of the night. He even said that he wasn't the last one to see her, that her friend Pam Hupp had dropped her off at 7:00 that night. Investigators, however, were fixated on Russ' guilt and disregarded any alternative explanations.

Knowing Pam Hupp was the last person to see Betsy alive, she was brought in for questioning as well. Pam told detectives that Betsy had openly expressed her desire to relocate to Lake St. Louis. She said that Betsy had told her she had planned to talk to Russ about it that evening but knew he would be angry. Pam painted a dark picture of Russ and made sure detectives knew that he was known for his violent temper. She claimed Betsy had considered leaving him.

Pam told investigators,

> "He started playing this game of putting a pillow over her face… to see what it would feel like… this is what it's gonna feel like when you die, or whatever, and act like he was kidding."

> "He makes comments about how much money he'll have when she's gone because he's got—this is what she said. I don't know for sure because I haven't seen their financials—but he's got life insurance on her at work."

Pam even told investigators to look on Betsy's laptop, and they'd find a letter that Betsy had written stating that she was afraid Russ was going to kill her. When they found the document, it also stated that Betsy had asked Pam to help her change her life insurance policy out of Russ' name and into Pam's.

When questioned about why Betsy would make Pam the sole beneficiary of her life insurance policy, Pam explained that Betsy had entrusted her to place it in a trust for her daughters, intending to give it to them when they reached the age of eighteen.

Pam initially agreed to take a polygraph test but later hired a lawyer who advised against it. Pam claimed she had previously sustained head injuries that may affect the outcome.

On January 4, 2012, Russ Faria was charged with first-degree murder and armed criminal action.

It wasn't until the trial that questions began to arise about who else could have been responsible for Betsy's murder.

Despite the meticulous detailing of Russ' whereabouts that night, including testimony from four friends who confirmed his presence with them, cell phone records showing he was twenty miles away, video footage of him pumping gas and buying items at a store, and time-stamped receipts from his purchases, the prosecution argued that it was all an elaborate conspiracy.

Even though Russ had no blood on him when Emergency Services arrived, and Pam was the last one to see Betsy alive, the prosecution suggested Russ' friends conspired with him to commit the murder.

The prosecution alleged his friends had held his phone while he killed Betsy and posed as him in shops to falsify his alibi. The prosecution portrayed Russ as a calculated murderer, driven by greed for Betsy's life insurance payout, unaware that she had changed the beneficiary to her best friend. Despite the prosecution's claims that Russ' friends had conspired with him in the murder, no charges were brought against them.

To make matters worse for his defense, the judge at Russ' trial prohibited his lawyers from implicating Pam Hupp in the murder despite evidence from her phone records indicating she was near Betsy's house for over thirty minutes after she claimed she had dropped her off. Furthermore, the defense was prohibited from mentioning that Pam Hupp was the sole beneficiary of Betsy's life insurance policy, which had been changed just five days before her death.

Additionally, the document found on Betsy's laptop that insinuated Russ could be violent was found to have been created using Microsoft Word 97—software that was not installed on that computer. It was also the only document with an "unknown" author found on that computer. This discovery hinted that the document may have been planted in an attempt to frame Russ.

Despite all the evidence exonerating Russ Faria, the prosecution convinced the jury of his guilt. In November 2013, Russ was convicted of first-degree murder and sentenced to life in prison plus thirty years without the possibility of parole.

―――――

For several years, Pam had played a role in caring for her mother, Shirley Neumann, who suffered from advanced dementia and arthritis.

After her husband's passing, Shirley moved into a third-floor apartment at Lakeview Park independent senior living community, allowing her to enjoy retirement without the burden of home upkeep. Shirley's family found peace knowing she was safe and well cared for in her new environment. At seventy-seven years old, Shirley, a proud retired schoolteacher, found joy in seeing her children, grandchildren, and great-grandchildren.

Despite living in a senior facility, Shirley thrived in an independent apartment, needing only occasional support. Pam visited regularly, assisting with meals and cleaning, as well as offering companionship.

―――――

Less than a month before Russ' conviction was handed down, Shirley spent the night at Pam's house following a hospital appointment on October 30, 2013.

When Pam dropped Shirley off at her retirement home that afternoon, she informed the staff that her mother wasn't feeling well and wouldn't be showing up for dinner that night or breakfast the next morning. Pam asked the staff not to disturb her mother and just let her rest.

———

The next day, at 2:30 p.m. on October 31, Shirley Neumann's body was found on the pavement beneath the balcony of her third-floor apartment.

Police discovered the open patio doors, with six of the aluminum railing bars bent and broken. Despite finding eight times the typical dose of Ambien in Shirley's blood, her death was quickly ruled accidental.

Once again, Pam was the last person to see Shirley alive. Once again, she stood to benefit substantially from the death. Pam was set to inherit five hundred thousand dollars from her mother's investments and life insurance policy after the accidental death.

———

In hindsight, it's easy to see that Pamela Hupp had an unquenchable thirst for money and was willing to go to extreme lengths to obtain it. Her actions revealed her manipulative and greedy nature, as she would stop at nothing to get what she wanted. Tragically, after murdering her best friend and mother, it appears that Pam's thirst for wealth was far from satiated.

During Russ Faria's trial, Pam was questioned about the delay in establishing a trust with the $150,000 in life insurance money she had promised to set up for Betsy's daughters.

Pam claimed she had been unable to set up the trust due to her mother's recent death from Alzheimer's disease. She had lied under oath, as Pam's mother had actually died from injuries sustained in the fall and not Alzheimer's itself.

Under scrutiny from Betsy's family and the wider community, Pam eventually transferred $100,000 into a trust fund for the Faria daughters. This transfer took place just one week before Russ Faria's trial began. The timing struck many as suspect, as if Pam was trying to deflect attention from her own possible involvement in Betsy's death.

As for the remaining $50,000 from the life insurance payout, Pam offered various explanations. She initially claimed she was using the money to assist the twelve-year-old daughter of a friend who had died. Later, she admitted this was a lie to placate people who kept inquiring about how she was spending Betsy's insurance money.

In reality, Pam had used funds to purchase a new four-bedroom house. When questioned about the source of the money for the home, Pam claimed it came from cashing in her own retirement accounts, not Betsy's insurance payout.

Matters came to a head in 2014, when Betsy's daughters filed a civil suit against Pam Hupp over the life insurance funds.

The suit aimed to recover the money they believed was rightfully theirs per their mother's wishes.

During a deposition for this lawsuit, Pam made a shocking admission: She had emptied out the trust fund mere weeks after Russ Faria's conviction. Pam stated that since it was a revocable trust, she had simply revoked it, implying the money now belonged to her. This revelation stunned Betsy's family, who couldn't believe Pam would so brazenly violate her friend's dying wish.

In February 2015, Russ Faria was granted a new trial based on several key pieces of evidence that had been excluded from the original proceedings. These included information about Pam Hupp being the beneficiary of Betsy's life insurance policy and her numerous inconsistent statements to the police.

On November 3, 2015, after spending almost three years behind bars, Russ Faria's retrial began. Over the course of the proceedings, his attorney presented a compelling case for Russ' innocence, highlighting the many inconsistencies in Pam Hupp's story and the lack of physical evidence tying Russ to the crime.

On November 6, after a bench trial in which the judge heard all the evidence, Russ Faria was acquitted of all charges related to his wife's murder. The courtroom erupted in tears of joy and relief as the verdict was read. After years of proclaiming his innocence, Russ was finally a free man. Pamela Hupp, however, knew her time was running short; if she didn't act fast, it would all be over.

On August 16, 2016, nine months after Russ Faria's release from prison, Pam Hupp called 911 from her home phone.

 "Hey, hello? Someone broke into my house. Help!"

"No, I'm not getting in the car with you. Get out! Get out! Get out!"

Immediately afterward, the call recorded several gunshots.

However, there was an unusual quality to her voice during the call. Despite claiming to be in a life-threatening situation, her tone lacked emotion. It was almost as if she were reciting from a rehearsed script. When she uttered, "No, I'm not getting in the car with you," it sounded as though she were narrating a story.

When officers arrived at the scene, they were greeted by a visibly shaken Pam Hupp. She told them that she had been the victim of a home invasion and had shot the intruder in self-defense. Inside the house, police found the body of thirty-three-year-old Louis Gumpenberger, who had been shot five times.

According to Pam's initial account, she had just returned home from running errands when Louis, who she didn't know, approached her vehicle in the driveway. She claimed he was armed with a knife and demanded she take him to the bank to withdraw "Russ' money."

Pam told police that she had managed to knock the knife away and escape into the house, but Louis had followed her inside. Fearing for her life, she had retrieved a revolver from her bedroom and shot Louis Gumpenberger five times, killing him. She said the driver of the car that had dropped Louis off looked like Russ Faria.

As investigators began to process the crime scene and dig deeper into Pam's story, several inconsistencies and suspicious details emerged. First, they discovered that Louis Gumpenberger had severe physical and mental disabilities stemming from a traumatic brain injury he had suffered in a car accident years earlier. He walked with a pronounced limp and had difficulty using his left hand, raising doubts about his ability to carry out the type of attack Pam described.

Moreover, police found a note in Louis' pocket that appeared to outline a kidnapping and murder plot targeting Pam. The note instructed Louis to kidnap Pam, force her to withdraw money from the bank, and then kill her, leaving the knife in her neck. It also mentioned hiding the money in a specific location and made reference to "Russ' money." To investigators, the note seemed almost too perfectly tailored to support Pam's story.

As they continued to gather evidence, detectives uncovered even more alarming information. They learned that just six days before the shooting, a woman had filed a police report claiming that a blonde woman matching Pam's description had approached her with a strange request. She said the blonde woman introduced herself as "Cathy" and claimed to be a producer for the television show *Dateline*. She said the woman had offered her $1,000 to record a scripted 911 call for a segment on the show. The woman found the request suspicious and declined her offer.

The incident bore a chilling resemblance to Pam Hupp's 911 call on the day of the shooting. Video footage taken from the woman's home security camera showed Pam Hupp speaking to her from the window of her SUV.

Further investigation of Pam's cell phone data revealed that she had been in Louis Gumpenberger's neighborhood less than an hour before the shooting, contradicting her claim that she had never met him before.

Investigators also found nine crisp, new $100 bills in Louis Gumpenberger's pocket, with serial numbers arranged in sequential order. Further bills discovered in Pam Hupp's possession followed the same sequential order. It was clear to investigators that Pam had either paid Louis or planted the bills on him after killing him.

Investigators also discovered that Pam had purchased the knife Louis held at a dollar store, and the paper note in his pocket was written on a notepad in Pam's house.

As the evidence mounted, a darker picture began to emerge. Prosecutors theorized that Pam had deliberately lured Louis Gumpenberger to her home with the intention of killing him and staging the scene to look like a botched robbery. They believed her ultimate goal was to frame Russ Faria for the crime, hoping to deflect suspicion from herself as pressure mounted over her potential involvement in Betsy Faria's death.

Pam Hupp was arrested on August 23, 2016, and charged with first-degree murder and armed criminal action in connection with Louis Gumpenberger's death.

After her arrest, Pamela Hupp was brought into an interrogation room for questioning. However, while detectives were out of the room, she snuck a ballpoint pen from the table into her pants. She then asked to go to the restroom. When investigators escorted her there, she began stabbing herself in the neck and wrists with the pen.

Pam's unsuccessful suicide attempt garnered little sympathy from prosecutors, who labeled her actions as the desperate acts of a killer.

In January 2017, Pam pleaded not guilty to her charges; prosecutors announced their intention to seek the death penalty. They cited Pam's selection of Louis as a victim, emphasizing his particular vulnerabilities.

Prosecutors could no longer dismiss the suspicion surrounding her association with the deaths of Betsy Faria and Shirley Neumann. Consequently, police reopened investigations into both cases. With the possible involvement of Pamela Hupp, Shirley Neumann's cause of death was changed from accidental to undetermined.

In 2018, the judge presiding over Louis Gumpenberger's murder case ruled that prosecutors could not introduce information about Shirley Neumann's death in the trial against Pam Hupp. However, evidence relating to Betsy Faria's death was allowed.

Pamela Hupp's trial for the murder of Louis Gumpenberger was scheduled for June 2019, but just before it began, she entered an Alford plea.

Although not admitting guilt, an Alford plea acknowledges that the evidence against her would likely lead to a conviction. This decision meant that Pam would not face trial for Louis' death, and as part of the plea agreement, the death penalty would be off the table. She was sentenced to life in prison.

Pam told her husband from jail that she chose the Alford plea option to spare her children from witnessing an ugly trial.

Following the plea, the Lincoln County prosecutor announced the reopening of the investigation into Betsy Faria's death.

In 2021, Pamela was interviewed as a suspect in connection with the murder of Betsy Faria for the first time.

Less than four days after this interview, she was charged with first-degree murder and armed criminal action, mirroring the charges brought against Russ nearly ten years earlier.

Pam Hupp entered a plea of not guilty, and the prosecutor declared his intention to seek the death penalty, citing the heinousness and depravity of the crime as well as Pamela's attempts to shift blame onto Betsy's husband.

Pam Hupp is scheduled to face trial for the murder of Betsy Faria in 2025. At the time of writing, no criminal charges have been filed in the death of Pam's mother, Shirley Neumann.

In January 2018, attorneys representing Russ Faria deposed Hupp as part of his lawsuit against Lincoln County. She declined to answer ninety-two questions regarding the killing of Betsy Faria. In March 2020, Russ received a $2,000,000 settlement in his civil rights case against the prosecuting attorney and three sheriff's deputies, who he claimed fabricated evidence, ignored exonerating evidence, and failed to investigate the other obvious suspect.

CHAPTER 8
THE CITY PLANNER

In late October 1981, Tina Marie Harmon stood outside the Union 76 Truck Stop in Lodi, Ohio, smoking cigarettes with three friends between rounds of playing Ms. Pac-Man. It was a typical after-school activity for the rebellious twelve-year-old.

Just after 6:30 that night, Tina and her friends decided to walk to a friend's house in nearby Creston, where they planned to spend the night, stay up late, play games, and talk about boys. As they walked, however, Tina decided she wanted a fudgesicle. She told her friends to keep walking the few remaining blocks, and she would catch up after going to the nearby convenience store. Tragically, Tina never arrived.

When police in the small town of Creston asked the store clerk if he recalled seeing Tina that evening, he said she bought her ice cream and went on her way. He hadn't noticed anything out of the ordinary—other than the scruffy older man in a jean jacket who had followed as she left the store. Sadly, the store clerk couldn't remember any details of the man.

Police searched throughout the night, but there was no sign of Tina. The next morning, various branches of law enforcement from the surrounding towns organized search crews to scour the area around Creston. News helicopters from Akron assisted in aerial scans while volunteers on ATVs scoured the area, yet no trace of Tina was found.

Police spoke to her friends, parents, teachers, and boyfriend for clues, but nothing helped. By all accounts, the girl, while rebellious, had no reason to run away from home. It was obvious she had been kidnapped.

Five days later, all hopes of locating the girl alive were squashed. Tina Marie Harmon's body was found in a field almost forty miles away in Navarre, Ohio. A man hunting deer found her fully clothed near an abandoned oil well.

The medical examiner reported that tears inside the young girl's vagina indicated that she had been violently raped. Bruises on her face and arms told a story of severe beating, and ligature marks on her wrists and ankles showed that her assailant had bound her. Ultimately, she had died from manual strangulation. The killer had initially tried to strangle her with a rope before crushing her throat with his bare hands.

Investigators found semen on her dress and panties, but DNA analysis was a long way off in 1981. They determined that Tina had died several days before, but her body hadn't been by the oil well the previous day. They believed the killer had kept her in his house or car for several days before dumping her body.

One piece of evidence stuck out to investigators: The body was covered in dog hairs and tiny, bright-orange fibers. The fibers were triangular or trilobal, which typically indicated they were carpet fibers. Still, without something to compare them to, the evidence was of no value.

―――――

The murder was eerily similar to the murder of fourteen-year-old JoAnne Hebert eighty-five miles away. Just three months before Tina's murder, JoAnne Hebert, a quiet freshman at Dublin High School in Delaware, Ohio, had ridden her ten-speed bicycle to Tag's Market to buy a soda. She was last seen using the payphone outside the market. When the store closed at 8:00 p.m., her bicycle was still by the phone, unlocked.

Two months later, a squirrel hunter found her body just a mile from her home. She, too, had been sexually assaulted and savagely beaten to death.

Just thirty miles further south, another young girl, nineteen-year-old Robin Durrer, had been found raped and beaten to death only 100 yards from her house that September. Police, however, were unable to link the three crimes.

―――――

Police investigating Tina Marie Harmon's murder were eager to identify a suspect. They briefly considered her father and later her teenage boyfriend, but both were swiftly ruled out as suspects.

On November 17, police finally received what seemed like a useful tip. A mother and daughter had watched as a young girl was trying desperately to get away from two "scruffy-looking" men in a beat-up car. When the mother honked her horn to distract the men, it gave the girl a chance to run away, but the men took a U-turn and chased after her. The mother and daughter hadn't thought to call the police until they saw the news of Tina Harmon's abduction on the television.

Unfortunately, the pair couldn't remember any specifics about the car, but after the mother underwent hypnosis, she claimed to recall some details. She said the car was a greenish-blue Pontiac or Plymouth with a red stripe down the side. She also recalled that it was missing its rear bumper and had fake blue fur lining the rear window.

Police interviewed a young girl who lived near the location of the alleged altercation and said the "scruffy man" description sounded like a part-time fruit picker who worked nearby.

Desperate to find the killer, police quickly focused on two potential suspects—the fruit picker, twenty-six-year-old Herman Ray Rucker, and his friend Ernest Holbrook Jr.

Herman Rucker had a rap sheet of various misdemeanors and a recent DUI. Holbrook was just nineteen but married with a child on the way.

Rucker's car, however, was nothing like what the mother had described. He drove a red Chevy Nova with a black hood, lacking blue fur on the back window. The rear bumper was fully intact.

Additionally, both young men had solid alibis: Rucker was with his family when Tina had disappeared, and Holbrook was attending his sister's wedding. Nevertheless, investigators still zeroed in on them as the main suspects in the murder case.

The case took a turn, however, when Susan Sigler, an acquaintance of Ernest Holbrook, contacted the police. Sigler claimed that she, Rucker, and Holbrook had been drinking at her house when they admitted they had kidnapped, raped, and murdered Tina Harmon.

Sigler told police the two young men said they made sexual advances toward Tina, but when she turned them down, they tore her clothes off, raped her, and then beat her to death by slamming her head against the car.

The problem with her story, however, was that the medical examiner found no damage to Tina's head. She had died from manual strangulation.

Sigler had also told investigators that Rucker had borrowed money from her so he could get out of town after the killing, but Rucker's employer showed that he hadn't left town. He had worked his normal hours both before and after the killing.

Susan Sigler told police that Holbrook's cousin, Curtis Maynard, had also heard the conversation and could back up her claims. Twenty-four-year-old Curtis Maynard had an IQ of not much more than a third grader, accompanied by an extensive criminal history of burglary and larceny. When he spoke to police on December 10, he was out on parole after being convicted of aggravated assault and grand theft auto.

Police, who knew Maynard was scared to death of going back to prison, told him that if he didn't assist them with their investigation, he could go back to prison for up to twenty years. Under oath, he repeated the same story that Susan Sigler told police.

> "Ernie and Herman was kissing on this girl and she didn't want them to. So they got mad and ripped her clothes off of her, and he told me he killed her."

One month later, Curtis Maynard was arrested again for theft. The charge meant he was going back to prison for the next four years. Desperate to stay out of prison, Maynard's story about the killing changed. This time, he claimed that Rucker and Holbrook had shown him Tina's body in a shed that had orange carpeting inside.

This was precisely the information the police were hoping for. They were aware of a shed with orange carpeting and had suspected it as the murder scene. However, upon analysis, the orange carpeting didn't match the orange fibers discovered on Tina's body.

The lack of evidence didn't matter to the police, though. They were desperate for an arrest so they could put the citizens of Creston at ease. On February 10, 1982, Herman Rucker and Ernest Holbrook were arrested and charged with two counts of aggravated first-degree murder, felony murder, kidnapping, and rape.

Rucker and Holbrook were tried separately. Both Rucker and Holbrook passed lie detector tests, and there was no physical evidence at all tying them to the murder. At both trials, the prosecution relied solely on the testimony of Susan Sigler and Curtis Maynard.

Although Curtis Maynard's story varied greatly and his criminal history was well-known, the jury believed that if he had seen the body at the crime scene, his story must have been true. On June 9, 1982, the jury deliberated for ten hours before they convicted Herman Ray Rucker of kidnapping, rape, and murder. Fifteen days later, he was sentenced to life in prison with no possibility of parole for twenty years. He was given an extra fifty years for the kidnapping and rape charges. Ernest Holbrook continued to sit behind bars awaiting trial and was faced with the same charges and potential sentence.

With Rucker and Holbrook behind bars, police and prosecutors assured the people of northern Ohio that they could rest easy. There was only one problem: Young girls were still turning up dead.

September 20, 1982, was the first day eight-year-old Kelly Prosser was allowed to walk home from school by herself. Two days later, her bruised and bloody body was found in Plain City, twenty-five miles from her home. She had been sexually molested, badly beaten, and strangled to death.

The case received extensive local media coverage and a large-scale investigation. Police interviewed numerous potential suspects and followed up on hundreds of tips, but none led to a conclusive identification of the killer.

Marshallville was a tiny town of less than 800 that was just a twenty-minute drive from Creston, where Tina Marie Harmon had been murdered. In July of 1982, while Rucker and Holbrook were still behind bars, eleven-year-old Krista Harrison and her friend Roy Wilson had been walking through the baseball fields collecting aluminum cans when Roy told Krista he was going to walk to the other side of the field to get some water from the drinking fountain.

Krista sat alone on the bleachers and waited for her friend when a maroon van parked on the street behind her. When Roy began walking back, he saw a white man with a mustache sitting next to Krista.

As Roy walked, he saw the man bend over to speak to Krista, then reach his hand up her blouse. Krista slapped his hand away, but the man put his arm around her and shoved his hand down her shorts. Roy began to run toward them as Krista tried to get to her bicycle, but the man grabbed her and pulled her close, whispering something in her ear.

Roy watched helplessly as Krista cried out while the man forced her into his van and drove off. As the van drove away, the man waved his arm out the window and shouted, "Bye, Roy!" before disappearing from sight.

Roy sprinted to Krista's house and frantically told her father what had happened. Without hesitation, Krista's father promptly contacted the police.

Roy provided the police with a detailed description of the kidnapper—a slender white male, aged between twenty-five and thirty-five, standing approximately five feet ten inches. He had dark curly hair and a mustache. He described the van as dark red or brown, with teardrop-shaped bubble windows on the rear panels and a roof vent on top.

Police quickly established roadblocks around Marshallville, and volunteers scoured the vicinity near the baseball park. Despite employing helicopters and sniffer dogs in an effort to locate the van, their efforts proved futile. The kidnapper and Krista had vanished without a trace.

At first, the police suspected that Krista had been kidnapped for a ransom, leading them to request the FBI to tap the Harrisons' phone line. However, as days passed without any ransom demands, this theory weakened. Krista's father made a heartfelt public plea on television, urging the kidnapper not to harm his daughter. Unfortunately, this plea also failed to yield any results.

After Krista had been gone for three days, the FBI delivered the devastating news to her parents that they believed their daughter was probably already dead. Despite extensive efforts, including searches in nearby woods and waterways as well as dragging the bottom of a nearby lake, no trace of Krista was found.

Six days after the kidnapping, Krista Harrison's body was found fifteen miles from Marshallville by a group of turtle trappers. She lay badly decomposed due to the summer heat and was positioned on her side next to a small, abandoned building. Clear plastic bags partially covered her body. Near the scene, investigators found a pair of black leather gloves, men's blue jeans, and a long-sleeve plaid men's shirt. A few miles away, searchers found a clump of Krista's hair that had been cut from her head, a Budweiser beach towel, and a large cardboard box soaked with Krista's blood.

An autopsy revealed the brutality Krista endured in her final moments. The coroner determined she had been violently strangled—the cause of death. Her body also bore evidence of traumatic sexual assault. Lacerations in her vagina indicated forcible penetration with a rigid foreign object, consistent with a vibrator or a similar item. Additionally, Krista had suffered vicious slashing wounds to her head, the blade cutting deep into her scalp. The depravity and violence inflicted on the young girl shocked even veteran police officers.

Investigators researched the origin of the cardboard box and plastic bag used to transport Krista's body. They discovered that both items were packaging materials for custom black leather van seats, specifically purchased from Sears.

What stood out most to forensic examiners, however, were the bright-orange trilobal carpet fibers found in Krista's hair and on the Budweiser beach towel found near the scene. Remarkably, these fibers perfectly matched the polyester fibers found on Tina Marie Harmon. This breakthrough prompted investigators to reconsider the charges against Rucker and Holbrook. It was clear the two cases were connected. Had they wrongly accused the two men?

Just days after Krista Harrison's body was recovered, Curtis Maynard changed his story once again. He recanted his testimony against Rucker and Holbrook and claimed he had made the story up because he was afraid he would be sent back to prison. He also claimed police had coerced him into testifying.

Officers who had handled the case denied Maynard's accusations but arrested him all the same and charged him with lying under oath.

Ernest Holbrook's defense attorneys were thrilled by Maynard's recantation, as it solidified their belief that Holbrook and Rucker were innocent of Tina Harmon's murder, and the real perpetrator remained at large. However, they were disheartened to learn that the prosecution still intended to proceed with Holbrook's murder charge despite this development.

Despite forensic proof that the killer was still out there creating mayhem, a lack of physical evidence against Holbrook, and the fact they were now without Maynard's testimony, on August 26, 1982, after a ten-day trial, a panel of three judges unanimously found Ernest Holbrook guilty of murder, rape, and kidnapping based solely on Susan Sigler's testimony. He was handed the same sentence as Rucker—life in prison plus fifty years.

Defense attorneys for both men tirelessly pursued appeals of their sentences. A month later, on September 15, 1982, Rucker was granted a new trial scheduled for June 6, 1983. While Herman Rucker received a second chance, Ernest Holbrook wasn't as fortunate—in January 1983, a three-judge panel rejected his plea for a new trial, citing inadequate evidence.

At Rucker's second trial, his lawyers focused on the orange carpet fibers that were found on the bodies of both victims. The fibers couldn't be tied to Rucker in any way, and it was clear there was still a killer on the loose. His lawyers also argued that Susan Sigler was an unreliable witness, having filed a false rape report in another county. Ultimately, on June 15, 1983, the jury agreed with the defense and overturned his conviction. After spending a year behind bars for a crime he didn't commit, Herman Ray Rucker was a free man.

———

Ten days after Rucker's release from prison, ten-year-old Deborah Kaye Smith went missing after attending a street carnival in Massillon, Ohio, just thirty minutes from Creston.

Deborah, who had been diabetic since the age of two, required two types of insulin daily. Concern heightened among authorities when she remained missing for several days, as they knew that without her medication, she could lapse into a diabetic coma.

Six weeks later, her decomposed remains were found by a canoeist along the banks of the Tuscarawas River. On her body, investigators found dried wax and the same orange carpet fibers found on Tina Harmon and Krista Harrison.

On October 17, 1983, twenty-eight-year-old Debbie Langford ran frantically down Symphony Lane wearing only a blue bathrobe. Her body was covered in blood. When she spotted a house with neatly trimmed flower beds in the front yard, she ran to the front door, screaming for help.

An elderly woman answered the door and could see the unmistakable look of terror and desperation on Debbie's face. Debbie's head had been shaved, and she was bleeding from several different places on her body. The woman rushed her inside the house, locked the deadbolt, closed the drapes, and called the police.

When emergency crews arrived, they found Debbie in a state of shock. Her arms and wrists showed that she had been restrained, and her left wrist was cut deeply and bleeding. Her entire body was bruised so badly that one of the first officers on the scene mistook her bruises for dark-purple underwear. She was burned from electrical shocks all over her body—but she was alive.

Debbie told police that she had no idea where she was. She said a man had abducted her at gunpoint from the gas station where she worked. She was taken to a house where the man had forced her to undress and tied her wrists and ankles to a weightlifting bench with rope and handcuffs.

The man had used a straight razor to shave her head. Over the next ten hours, he had subjected her to repeated rapes and beatings. He had then cut the wires of an electrical cord and used it to electrocute her.

The man had forced her to drink his semen and urine and used a plastic bag to suffocate her until she passed out—only to let her regain consciousness and do it all over again.

The beatings were so violent that Debbie could see her own blood splattered on the walls and even the ceiling of the room.

The man had moved her to a bed and retied her hands and legs to the bed posts, then put on a suit and tie and told her he was leaving for work. He would be back in three hours. He had told her if she tried to escape, he'd hunt her down and kill her.

Debbie told police she knew the man would kill her eventually anyway, so she'd pulled desperately at her restraints. After two hours, she had eventually worked one of her hands loose and untied her ankles. Her other hand, however, was handcuffed to the bedpost, and she had considered eating her thumb to get loose. Debbie had desperately tried to contort her hand so she could squirm from the handcuff. As the handcuff cut deeply into her skin, slippery blood had covered her hand, and eventually, she was able to slip out of the handcuff.

Debbie had wasted no time. She'd grabbed a blue bathrobe from the bathroom and ran from the house. Not knowing where she was, she had run down the road until she felt she was a safe distance from the house. When she had heard a poodle barking, she ran toward the house. Hoping someone was home, she had desperately pounded on the door and begged for help.

Police backtracked Debbie's steps to the house where she had been held captive and waited for the owner to come home. At 11:00 a.m., an official vehicle belonging to the city of Akron, Ohio, pulled into the driveway. When the man emerged from the car, Debbie positively identified him as her attacker.

Forty-three-year-old Robert Anthony Buell was a highly respected resident of Clinton, Ohio, who worked as a loan and grant specialist for the Akron city planning department. Buell was born in Cincinnati and had attended Norwood High School before serving four years in the Navy. At the time of his arrest, he was divorced with a teenage daughter and was dating a local attorney.

By all accounts, Robert Buell was a well-liked, college-educated, average man known for his sense of humor and charm. He often attended softball games with his girlfriend and was on good terms with his ex-wife and daughter, who initially helped raise money for his defense, not believing the charges against him.

Buell, however, had a hidden history of sexual deviancy and violence that his friends and family didn't know about. In 1978, Buell had been arrested for public indecency after exposing himself to a group of women. He was convicted on a misdemeanor charge of disorderly conduct, paid a fine, and had his criminal record expunged.

When faced with the charge of the kidnapping and rape of Debbie Langford, Robert Buell admitted his guilt and pleaded no contest. When authorities began investigating his potential involvement in other unsolved crimes in the area, even more evidence against him quickly piled up.

Just after his arrest, twenty-nine-year-old Patricia Lively from West Virginia told police she had been abducted by Buell while visiting Ohio. Buell had kidnapped her at gunpoint, then raped and tortured her for four days before releasing her. Inside Buell's home, FBI agents found the woman's clothing and a green long-neck bottle that he had used to sexually assault her.

Another woman came forward and told police that Buell resembled a man who had attempted to lure her daughter into his blue Ford Pinto. The woman had written down the license plate of the car, which investigators discovered was registered to Buell's ex-wife.

Investigators also learned of a thirteen-year-old girl who was sexually assaulted in the basement of her home by an unknown man two years earlier. For the next year and a half, she had received anonymous, threatening phone calls which were later traced back to Buell's home.

Several other reports surfaced from young girls who claimed that Buell had unsuccessfully attempted to force them into his maroon van.

When investigators started connecting the evidence from the murders of Krista Harrison and Tina Harmon to Buell, they knew they had found the real killer.

Robert Buell owned a reddish-brown 1978 Dodge van. The van, however, didn't have teardrop-shaped bubble windows on the rear panels, as Roy Wilson had told police. However, when they spoke to Buell's neighbors, they learned that Buell had recently removed the bubble windows and replaced them with rectangular sliding windows.

Even more damning was the carpeting inside the van. The van was covered wall-to-wall with bright-orange carpeting. Chemical tests matched the carpet fibers from his van to the fibers found on Krista Harrison, Tina Marie Harmon, and Deborah Smith's bodies. Investigators traced the carpet to a manufacturer in Canton, Ohio, who told detectives only 12,000 yards of the orange carpet were ever manufactured, and only seventy-four yards had been shipped to northern Ohio.

The van also had new custom black leather seats that investigators learned Buell had recently purchased from Sears. The packaging that was used to ship the seats was an exact match for the bloody cardboard box and plastic bag found near Krista Harrison's body. Buell had purchased the custom seats just three weeks before Krista's abduction.

Inside Robert Buell's home, investigators found five white candles and a sixteen-ounce carton of white candle wax that were similar to the wax found on Deborah Smith's body.

Investigators learned that Buell's dog had recently died, and he had buried it in the backyard. When they exhumed the dog's body and analyzed hair samples, they were an exact match for the dog hairs found on Tina Harmon's body.

Investigators discovered several cans of black spray paint in Buell's garage, which forensically matched the black paint found on the blood-soaked cardboard box used to transport Krista Harrison's body. Furthermore, detectives discovered that Buell had recently painted his house. The beige and blue paints from his house chemically matched paint smears found on the blue men's jeans recovered near Krista Harrison's crime scene. The jeans found at the crime scene were also the same size as jeans found in Buell's home and had the same wear patterns.

As investigators delved deeper into Buell's background, more unsolved cases emerged that they suspected he was involved in:

Damita Sullivan, a nine-year-old from Akron, disappeared in October 1981. Her body was found six months later, just a half block from her house.

Investigators also believed he was responsible for the deaths of eight-year-old Asenath Dukat in June 1980, eight-year-old Kelly Prosser in September 1982, and fourteen-year-old JoAnne Hebert in July 1981.

There was also the case of eight-year-old Tiffany Papesh, who had disappeared in July 1981 but was never found.

FBI agents believed Buell was responsible for two abductions and rapes that occurred in 1978 and 1979. In both cases, the women's heads and pubic hair were shaved. They were then blindfolded with a putty-like substance and held captive for more than twenty-four hours. One of the women reported being handcuffed, while the other was chained to rafters in a basement. Eventually, he dumped one on a rural road and tied the other to a tree before leaving her for dead.

The forensic evidence against Robert Anthony Buell was overwhelming, yet he denied killing Krista Harrison, Tina Harmon, or Deborah Smith. Regardless, on November 15, 1983, Buell was charged with the kidnapping, rape, and murder of Krista Harrison. Robert Buell pleaded not guilty, and the prosecutor announced he would seek the death penalty.

With all of the evidence of Tina Harmon's murder pointing squarely at Robert Buell, attorneys representing Ernest Holbrook filed a request for a new trial. Astonishingly, however, the Ohio Supreme Court still refused to clear the charges or allow another trial.

The Ohio Supreme Court, however, received tremendous backlash for its actions. Two months later, on January 24, 1984, they finally agreed to grant Holbrook a retrial.

On January 30, 1984, Robert Buell was sentenced to 121 years in prison for the abduction and rape of Debbie Langford and Patricia Lively after pleading no contest to the charges.

Buell stood trial for the murder of Krista Lea Harrison on March 19, 1984. Although the forensic evidence against him was irrefutable, Buell insisted he was framed.

After three weeks of testimony, Robert Anthony Buell was found guilty of the kidnapping, rape, and aggravated murder of Krista Harrison. Two days after his conviction, Buell was sentenced to death for the murder. He also received a life sentence for the rape and twenty-five years for the kidnapping, to be served concurrently with his death sentence.

Sadly, even after Buell was sentenced to death, Ernest Holbrook sat in prison for a murder he obviously did not commit. It wasn't until May 1984 that the state of Ohio finally dismissed all charges against him.

After spending two years behind bars, Ernest Holbrook sued the state and received $84,000 in damages for the wrongful conviction.

Robert Anthony Buell spent eighteen years on death row, during which time he filed numerous appeals and received several stays of execution. In January 1996, Buell was sent to the "Death House" at the Southern Ohio Correctional Facility, only to have a stay granted at the last minute.

Finally, on September 24, 2002, Robert Anthony Buell was executed by lethal injection. His final meal was a single black unpitted olive. Even hours before his death, Buell refused to admit his guilt. In a written statement, he wrote, "The citizens of Ohio have executed an innocent man. The prosecutor and judge know it."

Just before the needle entered his arm, Buell addressed the Harrison family, some of whom watched from behind the glass,

> "Jerry and Shirley, I didn't kill your daughter. The prosecutor knows that, and so do (Judge) Mark Wiest and (Prosecutor) Keith Shearer, and they left the real killer out there on the streets to kill again and again and again."

Tina Harmon's murder was officially solved eight years later, in 2010, when Buell's DNA was matched to the DNA found on her body.

The murder cases of Deborah Kaye Smith, JoAnne Hebert, Kelly Prosser, and Tiffany Papesh technically remain unsolved, but many in law enforcement believe Buell was the killer.

The murder of eight-year-old Asenath Dukat, previously thought to be another victim of Robert Buell, was officially linked through DNA to Brent Strutner in 2002, not Robert Buell.

CHAPTER 9
DEATH OF A CHEERLEADER

Elaine Sobek called her daughter, Linda, at 10:45 on the morning of November 16, 1995, as she did every morning. But on this occasion, Linda was in a hurry. She explained to her mother that she was on her way out the door for a photo shoot and would call her when she got back in the evening.

After she hung up, Linda changed the message on her answering machine:

> "Hello, it's Linda. It's 11:00 a.m. on Thursday, and I will be on location all day today, so I will not have access to a telephone. However, leave a message and I will call you back as soon as I pick the messages up this evening. Thank you for calling, and I will talk to you soon."

———

At twenty-seven, Linda Sobek embodied the image of a California girl, boasting a toned physique and cascading blonde hair. Among the volleyball players and rollerbladers lining the shores of Hermosa Beach, she fit right in—a natural match to the sun-kissed coastal scene.

When she was just twenty years old, her striking good looks got her a job with the Los Angeles Raiders cheerleading team, The Raiderettes. In 1992 she was named Raiderette of the Year.

Landing a spot as a cheerleader was just the beginning of Linda Sobek's vibrant modeling journey. Her phone constantly buzzed with offers ranging from gracing the covers of car magazines to swimsuit and lingerie modeling, and even some offers for nude modeling. However, Linda's true aspiration lay in the world of television and movies.

During the 1990s, Los Angeles teemed with young, beautiful hopefuls striving to break into show business. However, amidst the throng of aspiring talents, Linda stood out as someone destined for stardom, her trajectory unmistakably pointing toward success.

Although she loved the modeling world and had always wanted to be famous, she also looked forward to someday getting married and having children—which was ironic, because the next day, Friday, she was due to audition for a role in the popular sitcom *Married With Children*.

When Linda's mother hadn't heard from her that night, she called her apartment and spoke to her roommate, Bettye. Bettye was concerned that Linda had missed an 8:00 p.m.

appointment that evening. She was scheduled for a photo shoot for a calendar featuring 1940s-style clothing. Knowing Linda's dedication to her modeling career, it was puzzling that she hadn't shown up. Linda's boyfriend, who lived in Las Vegas, had also been trying to reach her all day, but calls to her beeper had gone unanswered.

Linda Sobek was street-smart and fully aware of the risks associated with being a model in Los Angeles. She was cautious about going on photo shoots with unfamiliar individuals or those who weren't reputable in the industry. That's why her friends were surprised when she didn't return home that Thursday night.

The following morning, when Linda failed to appear for her *Married With Children* audition, alarm bells rang for her mother. Sensing that something was amiss, she wasted no time in contacting the Hermosa Beach police to report her daughter missing.

In the bustling beachside community of Hermosa, disappearances weren't uncommon among the youthful crowd. Often, it was just a case of friends losing track of time after a night of drinking. However, Linda's absence had stretched to a concerning twenty-four hours. Without hesitation, the Hermosa Beach police notified law enforcement agencies throughout Los Angeles County, urging them to keep an eye out for Linda or her white 1992 Nissan 240SX.

Linda Sobek's fellow Raiderettes wasted no time mobilizing their resources. Leveraging their media connections, they swiftly spread the word. By Saturday morning, Linda's disappearance had become the leading story on every television and radio news channel in Los Angeles, drawing widespread attention to the search for the missing cheerleader.

Throughout the weekend, the police fielded an overwhelming influx of thousands of phone calls while Linda's friends tirelessly distributed over 50,000 flyers across Southern California. In a testament to their determination, the Raiderettes also rallied support, accumulating $20,000 in reward money for Linda's safe return.

―――――

Despite thorough interviews with Linda's closest friends, boyfriend, and former boyfriends, the police hit a dead end in their search for leads. Adding to the mystery, nobody seemed to know which photographer Linda might have met that Thursday morning. In an unusual move, Linda broke one of her own rules by accepting a job outside her modeling agency. Linda typically kept track of her modeling appointments in her day planner, but it appeared she had taken it with her, leaving investigators with little to go on.

―――――

Five days had passed since Linda Sobek's disappearance when the Hermosa Beach police received their first clue. Bill Bartling, unable to settle his outstanding traffic tickets with the county, found himself assigned to community service. A judge had tasked him with picking up trash from the garbage cans along the Angeles Crest Highway in the Angeles National Forest north of the city. While emptying the bin at call box number 309, Bartling noticed several 8" x 10" glossy photos of a stunning young blonde woman. Recognizing the girl's natural beauty, he tucked the photos in his backpack and continued picking up the remaining trash.

The following day, when Bartling saw the news that Linda Sobek had been reported missing, he immediately recognized the girl in the photos and called the Hermosa Beach police.

Early the following morning, detectives rushed to a ranger station deep in the Angeles National Forest to collect the remaining garbage before it was hauled away to the landfill.

Investigators transported four large rolling dumpsters back to Hermosa, where they emptied their contents for meticulous examination. Among the debris, they discovered several additional glossy photos from Linda Sobek's modeling portfolio, along with her missing day planner. Tragically, the page with her appointments on Thursday, November 16, had been torn out—a chilling discovery that led detectives to believe it was unlikely that they would find Linda Sobek alive.

Teams of searchers were dispatched to the expansive Angeles National Forest in a determined effort to locate the missing woman. Despite employing teams on horseback, tracking dogs provided with Linda's scent, and aerial search efforts using helicopters, the task of finding her amidst the vast 700,000-acre forest proved to be an exceedingly daunting challenge.

———

As detectives meticulously combed through the garbage retrieved from the four dumpsters, they stumbled upon what initially seemed like an inconsequential discovery—an owner's manual for an Oldsmobile Bravada. However, nestled within its pages was a one-page auto lease agreement that piqued their interest. The lease was for a Black Lexus LX450, a prototype SUV not yet available on the market.

The lease had been issued by Lexus Headquarters in Torrance, California, to a photographer from the Autoweek magazine for a photo shoot. Autoweek had hired a well-known and respected photographer named Charles Rathbun for the shoot, scheduled for an upcoming issue of the magazine.

What sent shivers down detective's spines was the contract date: November 16—the very same day Linda Sobek had gone missing.

Detectives quickly learned that Charles Rathbun had worked with Linda Sobek in the past, having photographed her for a cover shoot for *All Chevy* magazine. After checking his background, they also discovered a troubling detail: He had once stood trial for rape in Ohio. Rathbun was ultimately acquitted, however, after claiming the sex was consensual.

Detectives approached Rathbun at his home in Hollywood. When asked if he had any contact with Linda Sobek, he admitted he had. He told detectives he had met her at a Denny's restaurant in West Hollywood on the morning she went missing, just after he had picked up the Lexus SUV. But Rathbun claimed, after reviewing her portfolio photos, he had decided he couldn't use her for the photo shoot and the two had gone their separate ways.

When confronted with the discovery of the Lexus rental agreement with his name on it found among Linda's glossy portfolio photos in a trash can in the Angeles National

Forest, Rathbun offered an explanation. He claimed it must have been inadvertently mixed in with Linda's photos during their meeting at the Denny's restaurant.

Before leaving Rathbun's home, they asked him to come to the Hermosa Beach police station to make a formal statement. Rathbun agreed to come at noon.

Officers wasted no time following up on Rathbun's claim about their supposed meeting at the West Hollywood Denny's. When they arrived, they found Linda's Nissan, seemingly untouched since she had initially parked it there the previous Thursday.

When Rathbun failed to appear at noon as promised, the police grew suspicious. Detectives called, and Rathbun apologized for missing the appointment, assuring them he would be there by 2:00 p.m. Yet, once again, he failed to arrive.

Detectives, now wary, assigned a surveillance team to monitor his movements. However, when officers arrived at his home, they were met with a disturbing scene—Rathbun stood in front of his house, visibly intoxicated and brandishing a pistol. He was engaged in a heated argument with two women.

In a shocking turn of events, Rathbun fired a shot into the ground, resulting in a bullet ricocheting and striking one of the women in the shoulder. Both women, one of whom was a friend of his and a Los Angeles Sheriff's deputy, had visited Rathbun after he phoned them, drunkenly mentioning his involvement in Linda Sobek's disappearance.

When officers brought him to the Hermosa Beach Police Station for questioning, Rathbun's intoxicated state led to him vomiting on himself during the interrogation. His inebriated ramblings included vague admissions of involvement in Linda's disappearance. However, due to the failure of the officers to read him his rights before questioning, Rathbun's drunken confession was deemed inadmissible.

When Rathbun regained enough coherence to speak, he nervously recounted to detectives that it was all a tragic accident. He claimed that, following their meeting at Denny's, he and Linda had driven the Lexus to El Mirage Lake, a dry lakebed located in the central Mojave Desert, approximately 100 miles from Hollywood.

Rathbun told detectives that he had initially photographed Linda with the Lexus before suggesting she drive the SUV in tight circles while he took photos. When she struggled with the maneuver, he claimed he took her place in the driver's seat to demonstrate but accidentally struck her with the car when he lost control of the vehicle.

Rathbun said he panicked. He had considered taking her to the hospital but was sure she was dead. Instead, he told detectives he took her to a remote location in the Angeles National Forest, dug a shallow grave with his hands, and buried her.

Right away, detectives knew Rathbun was lying. Investigators had already impounded the Lexus SUV, and forensic teams found no damage to the exterior of the car. What they did find, however, was troublesome. In the back seat of the brand-new vehicle, they found a spot of human blood. Blood was also found on the car cover that was stowed beneath the floor in the back of the SUV.

Detectives escorted Rathbun to the desert, instructing him to lead them to the location where Linda Sobek was allegedly buried. Despite six hours of aimless driving through the desert, Rathbun claimed he couldn't remember where he'd buried her.

On Thanksgiving day, Charles Rathbun was arrested for murder, and a search warrant was issued for his Hollywood home. Inside, they found more than two hundred guns. They also found a duffel bag filled with rope, duct tape, guns, and an empty bottle of tequila. Detectives described it as a rape kit.

The following morning, detectives discovered Charles Rathbun had attempted suicide in his jail cell. He had asked an officer for a razor to shave with, disassembled it, and slit his wrists. As he bled out, he wrote, "I'm sorry, I didn't mean to hurt anyone" in his own blood on the jail cell wall. Spatters of his blood covered the sink and toilet, but officers quickly discovered what he had done. As his wounds were shallow, they were easily stitched up.

Saturday afternoon, detectives had talked Rathbun into helping find Linda Sobek's body again, and they took a helicopter toward the desert. As several television helicopters followed them, Rathbun admitted that Linda wasn't in the desert, as he had told them before. He finally took them to a remote location in the Angeles National Forest, where he had buried her in a shallow grave.

Linda's family watched on television as news crews showed an aerial view of investigators unearthing her body. She had been buried for nine days, but due to the cold weather and high elevation in the forest, she hadn't decomposed at all, and rigor mortis had not set in.

An autopsy provided further proof that Rathbun had lied about hitting her with the car. There was no damage to her body consistent with a car accident. Instead, ligature marks on her ankles showed that not only had she been restrained, but she had violently tried to break free, rubbing her ankles raw.

Further bruising showed that her legs had been forcibly pushed apart and her wrists had been twisted. A wound behind her ear showed that she had been beaten with a blunt object. She had been violently sexually assaulted and forcibly sodomized, most likely with the barrel of a gun. Linda rarely drank, but her blood alcohol level was almost double the legal limit, leading investigators to believe the alcohol was forced upon her. Ultimately, petechial hemorrhages of her face, eyes, and lungs proved that Linda Sobek had died from strangulation. The evidence revealed that someone had most likely been sitting on her back and forcing her neck into an object beneath her.

Strangely, Linda Sobek's body had been washed, her makeup had been removed, and she had been awkwardly redressed before being buried.

Tire tracks in the dirt near her body were traced back to the Lexus SUV, and blood and saliva in the vehicle were identified as Linda Sobek's.

As investigators discovered more evidence, Charles Rathbun's story evolved along with it. After the autopsy, Rathbun claimed that Linda had been drinking in excess during the photo shoot, and when he had accidentally hit her with the vehicle, he had laid her in the back seat of the Lexus. However, he said that when she had begun screaming and kicking at the SUV's interior, he had grabbed her feet and tried to hold her still to prevent her from damaging the car.

Rathbun claimed he couldn't calm her down. He claimed that, in an attempt to restrain her, he ended up on her back, inadvertently applying pressure that resulted in her accidental strangulation.

Of course, that didn't explain the obvious signs of rape or the deep ligature marks on her ankles.

At six feet three inches, Rathbun was a full foot taller and 100 pounds heavier than her. No matter how it happened, Linda Sobek didn't stand a chance.

By the time he went on trial for murder in October 1996, Charles Rathbun had changed his story yet again. He now claimed that he and Linda Sobek had engaged in consensual sex that day, but she was drunk, they had argued, and he had accidentally asphyxiated her. He claimed that he had nude photographs taken that day that proved his innocence.

While Rathbun sat in jail awaiting trial, he drew a map for his brother and told him to find five rolls of film that he had taken of Linda that day and discarded in the forest near where he buried the body.

Charles Rathbun's brother, Robert, found the five rolls of film after several months of sitting in the forest. However, instead of turning them over to authorities as potential evidence, he took it upon himself to have the film developed.

Four rolls of the film revealed Linda Sobek posing with the Lexus SUV at the El Mirage dry lakebed. However, disturbingly, some of the photos depicted Linda with torn stockings. Prosecutors raised concerns about whether Linda was being coerced into posing against her will.

The fifth roll of film, severely damaged by water and double exposed, contained eleven frames showing photos of a vehicle dashboard superimposed over close-up images of female genitalia.

During the trial, Rathbun's defense attempted to explain these photos as ones that Linda had willingly agreed to pose for that day. However, upon closer examination, it became evident that the model in the photos was not Linda Sobek, a fact further supported by a comparison with autopsy photos. Additionally, the dashboard photos did not match those of the Lexus SUV. Even if the photos had been of Linda, they were close-ups of genitalia only and in no way proved that they were taken consensually.

Witnesses who took the stand during the trial recounted Charles Rathbun's troubling history of hostility toward models he collaborated with, particularly expressing disdain toward blondes. One witness shared that after a previous collaboration with Linda Sobek, Rathbun had disparagingly referred to her as a "little bitch" and lamented about her being difficult to work with.

Prosecutors proposed that Charles Rathbun had propositioned Linda for sex, but she had rejected his advances. Enraged by her refusal, Rathbun hit her on the side of the head, twisted her arm, and tied her ankles to parts of the car's interior. He forced her to drink alcohol, then raped, strangled, and sodomized her using his gun. They believed he then washed and redressed her before burying her in a remote location in the Angeles National Forest.

As he made his way back to Los Angeles, Rathbun disposed of any incriminating evidence linking him to Linda Sobek, including her portfolio photos, day planner, and the photos he had taken of her that day.

After a five-week trial and six hours of deliberation, Charles Rathbun was found guilty of first-degree murder and sodomy. He received a sentence of life in prison without the possibility of parole.

After his conviction, Rathbun emerged as a person of interest in the murder of Stephanie Hummer, an Ohio State University student who vanished in 1994 and was found dead the following day from a blow to the head. Rathbun's father lived near her at the time. In 2006, however, DNA evidence proved that Jonathan Gravely had killed her.

Rathbun also faced suspicion in the 1993 murder of nineteen-year-old Rose Latimer, a model from Lansing, Michigan. At the time, Rathbun resided just blocks away from where the crime occurred. However, four years later, John Ortiz-Kehoe was convicted of the crime, shifting attention away from Rathbun.

The murder of Kimberly Pandelios in 1992, however, bore the most striking similarity to Linda's case. Like Linda, Kimberly was a stunning blonde with flowing hair, also known for her work in car magazines. Coincidentally, police received reports that Kimberly had met with an unknown photographer at a Denny's restaurant in Torrance, California. Tragically, days later, her body was discovered in the

Angeles National Forest, mere miles from where Linda Sobek's remains were found. For almost a decade, investigators suspected Rathbun could have been the killer. However, in 2006, David Rademaker was sentenced to life in prison without parole for her murder after DNA linked him to the crime. Like Rathbun, Rademaker had lured Kimberly to the forest for a photo shoot, then killed her when she turned down his advances.

CHAPTER 10
MOTHER'S DAY

In April 2017, Heather Suydam observed a startling shift in the behavior of her boyfriend, Joshua Webb. Something peculiar had transpired, altering him in a way she couldn't explain. While she didn't suspect drug involvement, Heather knew that Joshua's demeanor was decidedly off-kilter.

Several months earlier, Heather had uprooted her life and moved from the East Coast to the tiny town of Colton, Oregon, about an hour's drive south of Portland. She and Joshua shared a small barn-style outbuilding on the large rural property where his parents, Tina and David Webb, also lived.

By all accounts, thirty-six-year-old Joshua had grown up as a relatively quiet, shy young man who preferred his own company or that of a few close friends.

Early in life, he developed a vision problem which worsened as he got older. Although his exact diagnosis was unclear, his vision disability was substantial enough for Joshua to be considered legally blind and eligible to receive Social Security payments. This unfortunate disability made maintaining steady employment exceptionally difficult for Joshua over the years and contributed to his social awkwardness.

For the past year, however, Joshua had been prescribed antipsychotic medication after suffering from hallucinations and delusions where he was speaking to voices that were only in his head.

Despite the medication, Heather could tell he was going through changes unrelated to his vision. Joshua, who had never shown an interest in religion, suddenly described himself as "super religious." Although he couldn't pinpoint what denomination he was leaning toward, he knew that something had come over him and he was following the light.

Joshua also expressed discomfort about a feeling he was having in the back of his head. He described it as an "odd squid-pulsing sensation." He complained to Heather and other friends that a black box in his garage containing a device recording his every move and Fox TV "owned him." Joshua's statements seemed nonsensical, leaving his friends uncertain about how to interpret them.

Heather thought that Joshua's strange changes might be a result of his medication, or perhaps he wasn't taking his pills at all. However, in May, Joshua suddenly pushed Heather out of his life. He told her he didn't want to see her anymore without giving her a reason, simply instructing her to move back home to Massachusetts.

With Heather gone, Joshua told his sister and friends that he believed his girlfriend had been secretly injecting him with something—but he had no idea what it was. To his friends and family, it was clear that his paranoia had gotten out of control.

In early May, Joshua walked into the local police station carrying a heavy black duffel bag. He called for an officer to help him as he unzipped the bag to reveal it was full of guns. Joshua wanted to voluntarily surrender all the guns he owned, telling the officer that he was worried he could be a danger to those around him. He knew that the voices in his head were leading him into trouble.

On Mother's Day, May 14, 2017, Joshua's sister, Sarah, sent a message to their mother, Tina, letting her know she would be dropping by in the afternoon so they could spend Mother's Day together. But when Sarah pulled up in the driveway of her parent's house at 2:00 p.m., she noticed her mother's gold Chevy SUV was gone.

Knowing her father had left for work at 5:00 a.m., Sarah worried that her mother had forgotten about their afternoon plans. Thinking that maybe her mother had left her a note inside the house, Sarah walked up the front steps of the home, but her heart stopped when she saw the front door. The pale white paint of the door was smeared with what looked like blood.

Sarah pushed the door open and peered into the kitchen. Blood covered the floor. Frantically, she ran through the house, searching for her mother. In the room to the right of the front door, she found her mother lying on the floor in a pool of deep-red blood. Sarah was stunned by what she saw and instinctively knew there was no point in checking for a pulse.

Sarah rushed to a neighbor's house and called 911. When police arrived, they found an unbelievably gruesome bloodbath. Tina Webb had been fully decapitated, and her head was nowhere in the house. Blood spatter was found all over the house, covering the floors and walls. Bloody footprints and dog paw prints filled every room. Joshua Webb's dog, a dachshund named Cooper, lay on the kitchen counter with a knife still in his body. Several more knives and a large pruning saw lay on the counter beside the dog, all drenched in blood.

Next to Tina's body, officers found a large ceramic Incredible Hulk fist covered with blood. It appeared that Tina had been violently beaten with it.

Just as officers called for the medical examiner, another 911 call came in to dispatch. Thirteen miles northeast of Colton, in Estacada, employees of the Harvest Market Thriftway grocery store had a problem.

―――

After brutally beating and decapitating his mother on Mother's Day, Joshua Webb threw Tina's head onto the passenger seat of his parent's SUV, drove to Estacada, and entered the town's only grocery store.

Holding his mother's head in one hand and a large, blood-covered butcher knife in the other, Joshua walked in through the front door of the market, soaked from head to toe with blood. Terrified customers screamed and ran in every direction. It was a scene of chaos.

Still clutching his mother's severed head by her hair in one hand, Joshua used his other hand to grab a soda from the store cooler. After guzzling down the drink, he grasped the butcher knife again and walked toward the back of the store. His mother's decapitated head swung grotesquely from his grip as he moved.

Sixty-four-year-old Michael Wagner had worked at the Harvest Market Thriftway for years and thought he had seen it all. When he first saw Joshua, he didn't even notice the severed head. He only saw the knife and knew he had to act.

As Michael slowly approached Joshua, Joshua muttered, "You better run!" Before Michael could react, Joshua swung the eight-inch butcher knife he was carrying and violently attacked him.

Michael did his best to subdue Joshua Webb, but Joshua sliced him several times in the stomach and chest. During the melee, several other employees quickly rushed to help. Together, they wrestled Joshua to the ground and punched him repeatedly in the face. They managed to twist the knife out of his hands while other employees sprinted to the household goods aisle and retrieved a roll of duct tape to bind his hands and feet.

When police arrived, Joshua was under control, and a Harvest Market employee had placed an empty box over the severed head to hide it from the view of customers.

In the aftermath of the insane attack, emergency services quickly transported Michael Wagner to the nearest hospital, where he was immediately rushed into emergency surgery. Meanwhile, Joshua Webb was stripped down to his underwear at the scene, and police collected his clothes for evidence. He was then taken to the Clackamas County Sheriff's office, where he would be questioned in the death of his mother.

For the next twenty-four hours, Joshua remained eerily silent, his gaze fixed forward and seemingly unaffected by the detectives' inquiries. Described as catatonic and unresponsive, he only requested water, offering no further communication. He was briefly transported to a nearby hospital to address minor injuries sustained during the scuffle.

The next day, Joshua Webb suddenly announced that he had enjoyed a "nice nap" and was now prepared to talk. With a detached demeanor, he matter-of-factly admitted to the savage murder of his mother and the attempted murder of Michael Wagner.

Although he couldn't explain why he had done it, Joshua told detectives that he had beat his mother over the head with the handmade ceramic Incredible Hulk hand. During the attack, his dog, Cooper, wouldn't stop barking, so he tried to choke him to death. When that wouldn't work, he stabbed him repeatedly with a kitchen knife.

With a chilling level of composure, Joshua went on to tell detectives that he had retrieved a pruning saw from the garage, walked back into the house, and methodically sawed his mother's head off.

Again, he offered no rationale or motive as to why he took his mother's head to the Harvest Market and attacked the employees.

―――――

Michael Wagner managed to recover from his injuries, while Joshua Webb faced a litany of charges including murder, attempted murder, abuse of a corpse, assault, and animal abuse.

Joshua languished in jail, awaiting trial for over a year. Psychiatrists representing both the defense and prosecution assessed Joshua, diagnosing him with several psychotic disorders including schizophrenia. Their evaluations revealed that, despite a year of treatment with antipsychotic medication, Joshua still grappled with debilitating hallucinations, delusions, and auditory hallucinations, often engaging in dialogue with the voices he perceived.

Doctors concluded that Joshua had experienced a definitive psychotic break from reality at the time he attacked and killed his mother. His actions were consistent with someone completely disconnected from rational awareness or self-control.

His rapid descent into religious obsession, accompanied by perceived visions and full mental separation, signaled what one psychiatrist called "a perfect storm of his psychosis and fury," zeroing in on his mother as a target.

Joshua Webb entered a plea of guilty except for reason of insanity to all the charges brought against him on June 26, 2018. By invoking this plea, Joshua acknowledged that he had committed the acts in question but asserted that he was not legally responsible due to his mental state at the time of the offenses.

The resolution of Joshua Webb's case left the families of both Tina Webb and Michael Wagner struggling with a complex mix of emotions and frustrations. While they recognized the significant role that Joshua's mental illness played in the tragic events that unfolded, they struggled to come to terms with his sentence.

For Tina's family, the sheer brutality and savagery of her murder made it difficult to reconcile the lack of a definitive punishment. The idea that Joshua would be sent to a state psychiatric facility rather than facing a more traditional form of incarceration felt like an insufficient response to the heinous act he had committed. They grappled with the notion that the legal system seemed to prioritize Joshua's mental health over the need for retribution and justice for Tina's death.

Similarly, Michael Wagner's family experienced a sense of unease and frustration with the outcome. They felt that the Oregon statutes, which allowed for the insanity defense and the subsequent placement in a psychiatric facility, failed to adequately address the severity of Joshua's actions and the profound impact they had on Michael's life.

Both families expressed a shared concern that the legal framework could potentially enable Joshua, a deeply unstable individual who had committed such a brutal act, to one day walk free if doctors deemed his mental illness to be cured or sufficiently controlled.

CHAPTER 11
COLLATERAL DAMAGE

On a warm Sunday in late June 2014, Jennifer O'Brien drove ten minutes from her house, winding along quiet, suburban, tree-lined streets to her parents' home in the Parkhill neighborhood of southwest Calgary. It was the house where she and her four siblings grew up—a cozy split-level with a sprawling backyard.

Jennifer arrived with her two youngest boys in tow—rambunctious five-year-old Nathan, who was obsessed with superheroes, and his baby brother Max, not yet one year old. Her parents, Alvin and Kathy Liknes, immediately swept the kids into the bustling home.

Alvin and Kathy held an estate sale that weekend to sell off belongings before their upcoming move. After over thirty happy years in Calgary, they were finally retiring. They had purchased a smaller condo in Edmonton and planned to spend their winters in Mazatlán, Mexico, where they owned another condo. They were looking forward to relaxing in the sunshine and enjoying the next phase of their lives.

Jennifer and her parents had a very close relationship. She considered her mother her best friend. Her father, Alvin, was an entrepreneur who had achieved success through various business ventures over the years.

After spending the day with his grandparents, Nathan begged his mother to let him stay the night. Alvin and Kathy quickly agreed. They wanted to spend as much time as possible with their grandson before leaving for Mazatlán. Nathan was ecstatic when his mother agreed.

Jennifer had initially planned to stay the night, too, but as it got later, baby Max became fussy and had difficulty settling down. To avoid disturbing Nathan, Jennifer took Max home just before 11 p.m. while letting Nathan stay for the sleepover with his grandparents. Jennifer let Alvin and Kathy know she would return in the morning to pick up Nathan.

Just after 10 a.m. on the morning of June 30, Jennifer returned to her parents' house. With Max in her arms, she walked up the steps and found the door slightly ajar. She stepped cautiously inside and immediately noticed an overwhelming metallic odor. As she passed through the front foyer and into the living room, she was met with a horrifying sight—massive amounts of blood covered the floors, walls, and furniture.

Still reeling from the initial shock, Jennifer frantically searched room by room, calling out for her parents and young son. She navigated quickly through the chaotic mess of overturned furniture and scattered belongings. When she reached the basement, she found bedding soaked in blood. As she hurried to the upper floors, Jennifer noticed blood droplets and smear marks on the walls. It looked as though a bleeding body had been dragged down the staircase. A horrible sinking feeling came over her when she noticed a small, bloody handprint pressed into the wall, just a few feet above the floor.

But despite all the blood and gore throughout the house, there was no sign of Nathan, Kathy, or Alvin.

Having scoured every corner of the home, a panicked Jennifer rushed outside to call 911. Not knowing if the perpetrator was still in the area, the emergency operator told her to get in her car and lock the door until police arrived. Jennifer had to grapple with the unimaginable reality that her son and parents seemed to have been violently beaten and kidnapped.

When police arrived, they initially believed that Nathan may have witnessed the brutal attack and was hiding somewhere in the house, perhaps in a closet or cupboard. However, after a thorough search of the home, it was clear he was gone.

Sadly, a small tooth was found on the carpet that had obviously belonged to Nathan. The blood found throughout the house was analyzed and positively matched to Alvin, Kathy, and Nathan. To the investigators' dismay, however, after forensic teams scoured the house, they found no evidence left behind by the attacker. Whoever had taken the family hadn't left fingerprints or DNA. The only clues were several bloody shoe prints near the door.

Detectives noticed a lock on the side door of the house had been damaged. It appeared the intruder had drilled the lock and entered through that door.

Police immediately issued an Amber Alert for the missing boy. Police, along with Jennifer and her husband, Rod

O'Brien, held a televised press conference pleading for anyone with information about their missing family to come forward.

Numerous tips poured in from various locations across Calgary, and the police gathered CCTV footage from nearby residences and businesses.

Investigators speculated that the assault might be connected to the estate sale they had held over the weekend. It was conceivable that someone had observed an item of interest during the sale and returned later to steal it. In an effort to gather more information, the police urged anyone who had attended the estate sale to come forward with photos of their purchases.

A breakthrough finally came after four days with no sign of Nathan, Kathy, or Alvin when a tip emerged: A caller reported that they had seen a green Ford F-150 pickup parked on the street near the house on the night of the attack. Investigators meticulously sifted through hours of security camera footage until they stumbled upon video footage of the truck, which was subsequently aired on local news channels.

Shortly after the truck's footage was broadcast, the police received a call from Patty Garland, who said she knew who owned the vehicle. She identified the truck as belonging to her brother, fifty-four-year-old Douglas Garland.

Patty, who was married to Allen Liknes, the son of Alvin Liknes, had arrived in town to aid in the search for Alvin, Kathy, and Nathan. She was staying at her parents' residence, which was also where her brother, Douglas Garland, lived.

Douglas Garland was immediately brought in for questioning after being pulled over while driving the green truck.

Investigators began a search of the family's forty-acre rural property thirty minutes north of Calgary, where Garland lived with his elderly parents. After a thorough search, however, there was no sign of Nathan, Kathy, or Alvin.

Investigators did, however, find plenty of potential evidence. A duffel bag found in the house contained knives, batons, and several different kinds of handcuffs. On a patch of grass away from the house, investigators found a burn barrel with embers still smoldering in the bottom. Although detectives believed the barrel could have been used to burn evidence, initially they found only ash.

Over three hundred officers did a foot-by-foot grid search of the property, looking for any sign of the missing family—dead or alive.

On July 7th, Douglas Garland was arrested, but not on charges related to the disappearance of Nathan O'Brien and his grandparents. Instead, Garland was arrested for identity theft from a decades-old case. Back in the 1990s, he had assumed the stolen identity of a teenager, Matthew Hartley, who had died in a car crash.

Police held Garland in custody on the unrelated identity theft charge while they continued the search for Nathan and his grandparents. However, on July 11, he was released after paying a mere $750 bail. One strict condition of the bail was that Garland was prohibited from returning to his parents' farm.

Detectives believed that, despite the ban, Garland would eventually try to return to the farm. After his release, they set up a covert twenty-four-hour surveillance operation to closely monitor his activities.

Investigators continued their search of the Garland property. Hidden in the basement rafters, they uncovered a computer hard drive. When forensic teams analyzed the drive, they found that Garland had made several disturbing searches. He had searched "ways to inflict maximum pain through torture," "human dissection," "best blood removal solutions," and "optimal times to attack a victim at night." He had also searched how to pick a specific type of lock—the same lock installed on the Liknes' door.

The disturbing content of the hard drive also pointed to Garland's sexual interests: The drive was filled with images and videos of adults in diapers being bound and in simulated death scenarios.

In a basement office, Douglas Garland had books with titles such as *Handbook of Poisoning*, *Kill Without Joy—The Complete How To Kill Book*, and *The Death Dealer's Manual*.

Their continued search of the property uncovered more knives, more handcuffs, and several shackles—some of which were child-size. There were bone saws, guns, adult diapers, human teeth, and fragments of bone. They also found bloodstained shoe prints that matched those from the crime scene, a straitjacket, a set of prosthetic breasts, blonde wigs, eighty-nine pairs of both men's and women's shoes, racks of women's clothing in Garland's size, and meat hooks that contained the DNA of all three victims.

One shoe box found in Garland's closet was empty. Missing were a pair of size thirteen Dr. Scholl's tennis shoes. The tread pattern from the missing shoes matched the bloody shoe prints at the Liknes' home.

Upon closer examination of the ashes within the burn barrel, forensic investigators made a chilling discovery: a baby tooth, bone remnants, a pair of wire-rim glasses, and pieces of flesh.

One of the most damning pieces of evidence, however, came by chance. An airplane surveying the area in early July took detailed aerial photos every three seconds. On July 1, the photos shot over the Garland property showed three bodies lying on the grass. In the photos, two adult decapitated bodies wearing adult diapers were clearly visible. Nearby was the body of a young boy. The following day, the same plane took more photos, but all three bodies were gone.

Undeterred by his release conditions, Douglas Garland still attempted to return to the farm, just as investigators had suspected.

On July 14, shortly after 1:30 a.m., Garland was caught trying to sneak back onto his parents' farm, presumably to dispose of further evidence. Police helicopters using night vision cameras guided ground officers to Garland's location in the darkness. He was swiftly apprehended.

With considerable evidence against him, Garland was charged with two counts of first-degree murder for Alvin and Kathy Liknes, as well as one initial count of second-degree murder for five-year-old Nathan O'Brien. Although no bodies had been recovered, it was glaringly obvious they were dead, and the longest Amber Alert in Canadian history was officially discontinued.

With Douglas Garland in custody, detectives were able to uncover a potential motive for why he might have committed the murders of Alvin, Kathy, and Nathan.

In the 1990s, Douglas Garland was caught and charged with operating a methamphetamine lab on his parents' rural property. He was also charged with weapons violations and assault. To evade those charges, he fled to British Columbia and stole the identity of a teenager named Matthew Hartley, who had died in a car crash twelve years earlier. Garland lived under the assumed identity for seven years before being caught.

During his time in British Columbia, he worked at a chemical laboratory where he moved up into a management role. However, in 1999, authorities caught up with Garland about his drug and identity theft crimes. He pled guilty and was sent to prison, where he was diagnosed as mentally ill. While Garland was sentenced to thirty-nine months, he served only six months of his sentence. After his release, he moved back to Alberta to live with his parents.

Alvin Liknes and Douglas Garland were connected through Alvin's son, Allen, who married Garland's sister, Patty.

Eight years before the murders, in 2006, Alvin Liknes had hired Douglas Garland to help with a pump invention that Alvin had created for oil and gas exploration. The pump's function was to separate oil and water, and Alvin had hired Douglas to do some wiring for it.

Douglas Garland contributed to the project and expected to be credited as a co-creator when Alvin eventually filed patents related to the pump technology. However, Garland believed Alvin Liknes did not give him adequate acknowledgment for his contributions once the patents were submitted.

In early 2007, the business relationship further deteriorated when communication broke down, and Garland stopped responding to Alvin's calls. This falling out after their failed project collaboration left Garland harboring lasting resentment.

Meanwhile, through Douglas Garland's sister Patty's ongoing relationship with Alvin's son, he continued to hear news of the Liknes family over the years. Although Alvin never made any money from the pump invention, the constant family connection likely exacerbated old wounds for Garland, and the grudge continued to fester.

According to the investigators' theory, Douglas Garland's intended targets were Kathy and Alvin Liknes. Unfortunately, young Nathan's presence that evening as a sleepover guest was unplanned, resulting in him being collateral damage rather than an original target. Detectives concluded that Garland likely deemed it necessary to eliminate five-year-old Nathan, as leaving a witness at the scene who could potentially identify him would pose too significant a risk.

In January 2017, Douglas Garland stood trial for the murders of Alvin Liknes, Kathy Liknes, and their grandson Nathan O'Brien. Originally, Garland had been charged with two counts of first-degree murder for the deaths of Alvin and

Kathy, and one count of second-degree murder for Nathan's death. However, before the trial began, the charge related to Nathan's murder was upgraded to first-degree as well.

During the trial, Douglas Garland's parents took the stand as witnesses. They painted a picture of their son as a lonely individual who struggled to form friendships or meaningful connections with others. This characterization aimed to provide context for Garland's personal life and social isolation.

Garland's defense lawyer presented a key argument in favor of acquittal. He pointed out that the prosecution lacked any concrete forensic or scientific evidence definitively placing Garland inside the Liknes residence at the time of the murders.

The prosecution contended that Garland had meticulously plotted the murders for years, stemming from past failed business dealings with Alvin Liknes. Garland's internet search history showed he had researched that the optimal time to launch an attack was around 3 a.m.

According to the prosecution's theory, on the night of the murders, Douglas Garland first made his way into Alvin Liknes' bedroom, where he launched a brutal attack, violently bludgeoning Alvin. Garland then moved on to the adjacent room where Kathy Liknes and their grandson Nathan were sleeping. There, he savagely assaulted them, inflicting severe blunt-force injuries.

Investigators speculated that Garland had taken precautions to minimize leaving incriminating evidence at the crime scene. They proposed that he might have worn a protective Tyvek suit, which would have covered his body and prevented his DNA from being deposited in the home during the attacks.

Moreover, based on the evidence gathered, law enforcement officials concluded that Alvin, Kathy, and Nathan were likely still alive, albeit grievously wounded when Garland removed them from the house and loaded them into his truck. This theory was supported by the fact that multiple items discovered on Garland's property, including knives, bone saws, and meat hooks, bore the DNA of all three victims. Additionally, a pair of rubber boots seized from Garland's residence also tested positive for the presence of the victims' DNA.

On February 16, 2017, after five weeks of trial, Douglas Garland was found guilty on all three counts of first-degree murder. He received an automatic life sentence for each conviction.

In addition, the judge sentenced him to serve seventy-five years before parole eligibility. It was the longest prison sentence in Canadian history at the time. The sentence meant Garland would have to live to at least age 129 before being eligible for parole.

Garland filed an appeal seeking a new trial or a reduced sentence. In June 2022, the Alberta Court of Appeals upheld his convictions and sentence.

The horrific tragedy of losing Nathan left his parents, Jennifer and Rod O'Brien, searching for a way to honor their beloved little boy. Though the pain of his absence could never fade, they hoped to carry on his bright and enthusiastic spirit through an organization supporting causes Nathan would have loved.

In 2014, an anonymous $1 million donation helped launch the Nathan O'Brien Children's Foundation. Its mission focuses on aiding underprivileged and at-risk youth with financial assistance for sports, education, and leadership initiatives.

CHAPTER 12
THE SUITCASE KILLER

Melanie Lynn Slate was born in Ridgewood, New Jersey, on October 8, 1972, to Linda and Michael Caporero. She grew up in Middletown Township, New Jersey, with her parents and younger sister. As a young girl, she was a "Jersey Girl" through and through. With her tightly permed, curly, dark-brown hair, the petite girl always had a big, bright smile on her face.

Melanie was an excellent student. She was on the honor roll while at Middletown High School South and graduated at the top of her class in 1990. After graduation, she enrolled at Rutgers University with a double major in mathematics and psychology. There, she made the Dean's List for several semesters and graduated with honors in 1994.

After college, Melanie decided to focus on a career in nursing. She attended the Charles E. Gregory School of Nursing in New Jersey. Again, she excelled, graduating second in her class as a registered nurse in 1997.

The following year, Melanie started working as a nurse at RMA Associates, a fertility clinic in Morristown, New Jersey. By all accounts, she was a skilled, caring nurse who developed an excellent rapport with her patients struggling with infertility.

During her college years, Melanie had worked as a waitress in a restaurant and met William "Bill" McGuire, who worked at the same restaurant. Like Melanie, Bill was also working to pay his way through college.

Bill had a playful, joking personality and was known by coworkers as "the rude waiter" because he would hurry customers along, though always in a humorous manner. Melanie found an instant attraction in Bill's fun-loving and clever attitude toward life.

Bill McGuire was raised in the Bronx in New York City. After high school, he served several years in the U.S. Navy and remained good friends with some of his Navy buddies, particularly John Rice. After the Navy, Bill attended college.

Outside of work, Bill enjoyed the thrill of gambling. He often drove south to Atlantic City, where he had his favorite casinos and was recognized as a frequent patron. He also studied stock trading in his spare time and dreamed of making it big with a series of well-placed trades.

Bill and Melanie dated off and on for several years, but their relationship was tumultuous, to say the least. One minute, they'd be crazy in love; the next, someone would cheat, and they'd break up. Determined to make it work, Bill and Melanie always got back together, but the cycle was destined to repeat itself over and over.

Despite the volatility, after a few years of passion and conflict, Bill was convinced Melanie was his one true love and proposed in 1998.

At first, Melanie had some uncertainty. Bill had previously been married during his years in the Navy, but the relationship was short-lived. Additionally, he had a criminal record, having faced charges for a felony reckless driving offense.

Despite some family misgivings about Bill's judgment and reliability, the couple married in October 1999 in an extravagant wedding ceremony. However, relatives on both sides of the aisle had doubts about how long the marriage would last.

Just months after the wedding, Melanie became pregnant with their first son, who was born in the fall of 2000. By 2002, she was pregnant again with another boy.

Bill McGuire worked as a computer programmer for the New Jersey Institute of Technology, making a healthy $65,000 a year, while Melanie continued her work at RMA Associates during her pregnancy. They had moved to a townhouse in Woodbridge, New Jersey, to be closer to both of their jobs.

For almost four years, Melanie McGuire worked closely with a well-regarded doctor and partner at the fertility practice, Dr. Bradley Miller. The two had developed a close friendship over the years and felt extremely comfortable around each other, but they both knew it was more than a friendship.

Melanie was thirty-eight weeks into her second pregnancy and getting ready to start her maternity leave when she complained of neck and back pain after a long day on her feet. Inside his private office, Dr. Miller offered to massage her shoulders. In a matter of minutes, however, Melanie was on her knees, giving him oral sex. That initial sexual encounter in December 2002, just days before she gave birth, was the beginning of what would become a torrid three-year affair.

Dr. Miller was married with children, too, but despite their commitments, he and Melanie got together every chance they could. They secretly met for sex and, before long, had fallen deeply in love. Melanie and Bradley secretly talked about their plans for the future, including the possibility of getting married, having a life together, and having more children. However, neither was ready to leave their current spouses and tear apart their families.

As passion and promises unfolded behind closed doors, Melanie's domestic life with Bill grew increasingly strained. The year 2003 was marked by heightened tension, leading to frequent heated arguments between them. According to Melanie, the fights occasionally escalated into violence. Melanie showed an obvious lack of commitment to the relationship, prompting Bill to turn to heavy drinking and compulsive gambling. Desperate to get away from the house, Bill frequently made trips to Atlantic City, where he would disappear for days at a time. The endlessly escalating tension frequently triggered violent outbursts from Bill.

Melanie later recalled an instance when Bill had received a traffic ticket. After the police officer drove away, he called Melanie, screamed at her, and said he was going to come home and kill her.

In early 2004, after concealing their affair for years, Dr. Miller was prepared to end his marriage to be exclusively with Melanie. He became increasingly frustrated, however, when Melanie didn't show the same level of commitment. Driven by their shared dream of a life together, he couldn't understand why Melanie was hesitant. He started urging her to pursue a divorce.

Bradley's frustrations came to a head in late April 2004 when Melanie announced that she and Bill were due to close escrow on a new $450,000 house. Bradley was shocked. He couldn't understand why she had agreed to purchase a house with her husband when she claimed she was planning to leave him. Melanie, however, argued that Bill was squandering their money away in Atlantic City, and she wanted something to show for it if he lost it all.

On the afternoon of April 28, Melanie and Bill were handed the keys to their new house and planned to move in over the coming weekend. That evening, Bill McGuire sat on the couch with a bottle of red wine and called John Rice, his best friend from the Navy, to tell him the good news. Bill told John it was the happiest he'd ever been.

Later that night, while Bill was passed out drunk on the couch, Melanie called Bradley and told him that, yes, they had purchased the house, but not to worry—she would talk to Bill in the morning. She told Bradley she would confront Bill, tell him she wanted a divorce, and everything would work out fine.

However, things didn't work out as Melanie had planned. According to Melanie, Bill woke up at around 4:00 a.m. hungover and angry. He screamed at her that he felt like he was "settling" for a house he never really wanted in the first place. What he really wanted was to move six hours south to Virginia Beach, Virginia.

Melanie later said the argument became physical when Bill cornered her in the laundry room. Bill detested dryer sheets and believed it reflected that she was too lazy to put liquid fabric softener into the wash. Bill grabbed a dryer sheet, stuffed it in her mouth, and pushed it down her throat, all the while screaming at her that the sheets were a choking hazard for their children.

When Bill slapped her across the face, Melanie grabbed her two-year-old son, ran into the bathroom, and locked themselves in.

Over the next several minutes, Melanie listened from behind the bathroom door as Bill screamed at her and packed his bags. He shouted that he was leaving forever, and she would have to explain to her children why they didn't have a father.

Although he claimed he wasn't coming back, Melanie assumed Bill had driven down to Atlantic City as usual and would return after a few days. But this time, she was done. She was determined to leave him once and for all.

———

The next day, an email sent from Bill's Blackberry to his office said he was sick and wouldn't be coming to work. However, his office never received the email because it was addressed incorrectly.

That same morning, Melanie called an attorney friend who told her she should get a temporary restraining order against her husband.

On April 30, Melanie McGuire appeared before a judge and gave a sworn statement that she believed Bill posed a risk to herself and her children. As she presented her statements, the judge asked if the couple owned any weapons, to which she replied, "No. Not to my knowledge."

Several days later, when Bill still hadn't returned, Melanie sought the services of a divorce attorney. During their meeting, she expressed concern about not having heard from her husband for several days and inquired whether she should file a missing person report. The attorney, however, advised against it.

On May 5, Don Connors and Chris Henkle were on their boat heading out fishing near the Chesapeake Bay Bridge-Tunnel in Virginia Beach, Virginia. They had anchored the boat just off the Fisherman Island National Wildlife Refuge when they noticed a dark rectangular object floating in the water. Curious, they pulled up the anchor and motored toward the object. As they got closer, they could see it was a dark-green Kenneth Cole suitcase. Assuming it had fallen off a car going across the bridge above, they hauled the heavy bag onboard. Don Connor's young son was excited to see what was inside and quickly unzipped it. When Chris Henkle saw the black trash bag inside, he knew it was a bad sign. However, before he could stop him, the boy had ripped open the plastic bag to reveal a pair of pale-white, severed human legs.

When investigators arrived, they knew that if they had only found legs, there were most likely more body parts that would surface soon. They discovered the Kenneth Cole suitcase was one of a set of three, and they were on the lookout for the two remaining bags in the set.

Six days later, a young woman watching birds on the beaches of Fisherman Island came across another dark-green Kenneth Cole suitcase that had washed up on shore. The woman unzipped the bag and was instantly hit with the strong smell of decomposition. She quickly recoiled from the bag and called the police.

Inside the second suitcase, investigators found another black plastic bag containing a man's head, torso, and arms. The head had been wrapped in a white medical blanket with a logo reading "HCSC." The torso had two bullet holes in it, while a third pierced the head. Two of the three bullets were recovered from inside the torso. The man had been killed with .38 caliber wadcutter bullets, which were flat-fronted bullets designed for shooting paper targets.

A third dark-green Kenneth Cole suitcase, the smallest of the set, was found floating in the water in the same area on May 16. Inside, investigators found the rest of the body—the pelvis down to just above the knees.

On May 21, police released a facial composite sketch of the man found in the suitcases to the media. They desperately hoped that someone would recognize him.

―――

Almost a month after Bill McGuire had gone missing, his best friend's wife, Susan Rice, saw the composite sketch on the Virginia Evening News and immediately called her husband. Both John and Susan Rice had been worried about Bill, knowing it wasn't like him to be gone for so long. The sketch on the news gave Susan a sinking feeling of dread.

Initially, John wasn't convinced that the composite drawing was Bill, but after some discussion, the couple called the Virginia Crime Solvers tip line and told them to look into the disappearance of Bill McGuire.

Because of Bill's prior reckless driving violation in Virginia, his fingerprints were already in the state's database. When the fingerprints from the database were compared to the fingerprints taken from the dismembered body, they were indeed a match for Bill McGuire.

———

When detectives broke the news to Melanie McGuire that her husband had been murdered, she broke down sobbing. Although her tears seemed genuine, one thing struck detectives as strange: Melanie didn't ask how Bill had been murdered or what sort of condition he was in when he was found.

Detectives then let Melanie know that they would like to ask her some questions about her husband's disappearance and murder. She agreed to the questioning and showed up at the police station with two attorneys in tow. During the interrogation, detectives noticed her nervousness. Melanie's hands were shaking and she stumbled over her words, but she never shed a tear when speaking of her dead husband.

From the very beginning, every move Melanie McGuire made seemed like a clue that she had killed her husband.

When asked if she or her husband owned any matching luggage, she initially said they didn't, but when shown a photo of the Kenneth Cole three-piece set in which Bill's body parts were found, she suddenly remembered that the set was theirs.

When Melanie finally learned of the brutal manner in which her husband was murdered, she told detectives she had a likely theory. She suggested Bill's obsessive gambling had probably gotten him into debt in Atlantic City and that he had owed money to someone who may have killed him—maybe a loan shark or mobster.

She suggested that investigators go to Atlantic City to look for his car. Sure enough, days later, detectives found Bill's blue Nissan Maxima in Atlantic City.

During their searches of Melanie's new home and the apartment she and Bill had previously shared, detectives learned that she had already disposed of all of Bill's clothing. She had given it all away to her cousin. Upon locating the cousin, investigators found the clothes were still stored in black plastic trash bags that were identical to the bags containing Bill McGuire's dismembered body parts.

Forensic investigators thoroughly searched their Woodbridge Township apartment, believing Bill had been killed there. However, despite tearing out the walls, floorboards, and piping, they found no forensic evidence that Bill had been dismembered there.

Investigators then began looking into whether Melanie McGuire had any access to a gun. She had already stated that neither she nor Bill had owned any weapons, and searching gun record databases in both New Jersey and Virginia, they found nothing. But nearby Pennsylvania had more relaxed gun laws. When they checked records in Pennsylvania, they found that just two days before Bill McGuire had disappeared, Melanie had purchased a Taurus .38 Special and wadcutter bullets at John's Gun & Tackle Room.

Although caught in a lie, Melanie had a perfectly logical explanation for buying the gun. She claimed that she had purchased it for Bill because he couldn't legally buy a weapon due to his felony reckless driving conviction. She attributed the fact that the purchase happened just two days before Bill went missing to sheer coincidence.

———

The pieces really started to fall into place when investigators acquired a warrant to tap Melanie's phone calls. In just forty days, investigators recorded more than 500 hours of her phone conversations.

It was through these recordings that investigators quickly discovered she had been in a three-year affair with Dr. Bradley Miller. This new information provided a motive for Melanie to kill her husband.

When confronted, Bradley Miller insisted he had nothing to do with the murder of Bill McGuire. In order to prove his innocence, detectives asked him to assist with the investigation. Miller agreed to continue calling Melanie and to try to coax information out of her. Through the phone calls, it quickly became clear to investigators that Bradley Miller had nothing to do with the murder.

Despite listening to hundreds of hours of her conversations, Melanie McGuire never once broke down and admitted guilt.

Investigators then concentrated their efforts on tracking Melanie's movements in the days immediately after Bill's disappearance. Her E-ZPass toll records showed several trips to Atlantic City, Delaware, and Virginia in the days after Bill's disappearance.

On April 30, 2004, just two days after Bill went missing, Melanie used her E-ZPass to travel 170 miles south on the Garden State Parkway to Atlantic City. Melanie later explained that she went there to look for her husband's car. Miraculously, she immediately found the car in the sea of parking lots dotting the city. Melanie claimed she wanted to play a joke on Bill and moved his car across town to the Flamingo Hotel's parking lot so he couldn't find it.

Her explanation appeared ludicrous. Investigators couldn't understand why a woman who had just taken out a restraining order would travel so far to play a joke on a husband who she claimed was abusive. Instead, detectives believed Melanie was planting evidence. They believed she and an unknown accomplice had driven both cars to Atlantic City to make it look like Bill had traveled there.

Then, five days after Bill had gone missing, Melanie's E-ZPass showed she traveled 340 miles south to the Chesapeake Bay Bridge-Tunnel. In her recorded phone conversations with Bradley Miller, Melanie claimed she had traveled through the night to go furniture shopping very early in the morning in Delaware since the state had no sales tax. However, it appeared suspicious that Melanie later called E-ZPass and unsuccessfully attempted to remove the charges from her account history.

Prosecutors believed the trip was made late at night so she could hurl the three suitcases filled with her husband's body parts over the railing of the bridge. The first suitcase, containing Bill's severed legs, was found the very next day.

The evidence against Melanie McGuire continued to pile up. Further examination of the black plastic garbage bags she had used to give away Bill's clothing was forensically proven to have been manufactured within hours of the bags containing Bill's body parts.

Investigators found green fibers on one of the bullets recovered from Bill McGuire's body. Analysis showed the fibers were made of polyester fill—a common material in household items like pillows and cushions. The McGuires owned a green couch with similar fibers. Investigators theorized Melanie had used one of the couch's pillows or cushions to muffle the noise of gunfire.

Similarly, Bill's head was wrapped in a medical-grade blanket with a logo bearing the initials "HCSC" on it. The facility where Melanie worked stocked identical medical blankets. In fact, a witness later told police that Melanie had used the same blankets to protect furniture when she moved into the new house.

On the carpeting inside Bill's Nissan, investigators found microscopic bits of human flesh they referred to as "human sawdust." DNA analysis revealed that the flesh belonged to Bill McGuire. Experts theorized the bits were pieces of Bill that had been pulled from his body while he was being dismembered and then transferred to the carpeting from the bottom of Melanie McGuire's shoes.

The final nail in the coffin for Melanie McGuire was a syringe and a prescription bottle of chloral hydrate found in the glove box of Bill McGuire's abandoned Nissan Maxima. Investigators discovered the prescription for the strong sedative was written using Dr. Bradley Miller's prescription pad from the medical practice where both he and Melanie worked.

The prescription was filled on the morning of Bill's disappearance. Handwriting analysis revealed that Dr. Miller did not write the prescription; instead, it appeared to be in Melanie McGuire's handwriting. Moreover, the individual named on the forged prescription had never visited the pharmacy nor received the prescribed drugs.

By the time the chloral hydrate was discovered in the car, Bill McGuire's body had long since been cremated. When the medical examiner had initially tested the tissues and fluids in Bill McGuire's body, there was no indication that there were any drugs in his system. However, that toxicology test was only seeking evidence of more common drugs such as alcohol, cocaine, or opiates.

Still, prosecutors believed Melanie had stolen the prescription pad, forged Dr. Miller's signature, and used the drug to sedate her husband before shooting him three times and dismembering his body.

―――

Despite her insistence that all of the evidence against her was just an extraordinary series of unfortunate coincidences, Melanie McGuire was arrested for murder as she dropped her kids off at daycare.

―――

After more than two years of investigation, Melanie McGuire finally went on trial for murder on March 5, 2007. The intense media spotlight glared down. The case of alleged betrayal, brutality, and mystery had enraptured the public's imagination.

The prosecution's case revolved largely around the gun

evidence, computer searches, and Melanie's cell phone records.

They argued that all evidence pointed to Melanie. She had purchased a .38 Taurus revolver just two days before her husband's disappearance. The bullets found in his body were the same type that she had purchased. Although the gun was never recovered, the lands and grooves on the bullets were consistent with that specific firearm.

During the month before Bill's death, the McGuire's home computer was used to search terms such as "Undetectable poisons," "How to commit murder," "How to purchase guns illegally," and "chloral hydrate."

Melanie's cell phone pinged a tower in Atlantic City on April 30 at 1:00 a.m. In the same timeframe, Bill McGuire's phone was used to call their New Jersey apartment. This supported the idea that she had planted his car in Atlantic City.

The medical blanket found with Bill's body parts matched blankets from Melanie's workplace. Also, the luggage containing Bill's severed remains was the same brand and material as the set that the McGuires owned.

While complete physical evidence was lacking, prosecutors strategically lined up circumstantial forensic proof potentially linking Melanie to several aspects of the crime.

Melanie McGuire was upbeat and relaxed during the trial and seemed to enjoy being the center of attention. She dressed stylishly and hired Joe Tacopina, a high-profile attorney who had represented Alex Rodriguez, to represent her.

The prosecution argued that Bill McGuire's vicious killing was a methodically organized and meticulously planned murder. The defense, however, countered that argument by pointing out that if Melanie had indeed planned the murder so meticulously, she wouldn't have left behind evidence that directly implicated her, such as blankets from her workplace, a prescription bottle linked to her boyfriend, and body parts disposed of using her own suitcase set.

The defense argued that Bill McGuire had a serious gambling problem and could have owed tens of thousands of dollars to any number of loan sharks in Atlantic City.

Over the course of seven weeks, the prosecution presented eighty-one witnesses, including Melanie's boyfriend, Dr. Bradley Miller. Miller's testimony, however, was beneficial to both the prosecution and the defense.

His testimony and the recorded phone conversations showed the possibility that Melanie's motive for the murder was so she could be with him while avoiding a divorce and child custody battle.

However, Miller's appearance also shed light on flaws in his character, revealing that he was still engaged in an affair with Melanie McGuire during those calls.

Ultimately, the mountain of evidence pointed squarely at Melanie McGuire, and a jury found her guilty of first-degree murder on April 23, 2007. She was further convicted of perjury, desecration of human remains, and possession of a weapon for unlawful purposes. On July 19, she was sentenced to life in prison. She will be eligible for parole when she is 101 years old.

To this day, there are many who believe in Melanie McGuire's innocence. The fact that no one witnessed the murder, no murder weapon was recovered, and no forensic evidence conclusively tied her to the crime, some believe, left room for reasonable doubt.

Prosecutors, however, maintain their belief that Melanie McGuire may have received assistance. They doubt she had the physical capability to dismember her husband and dispose of three suitcases containing his body parts from the Chesapeake Bay Bridge-Tunnel by herself. They suspect Melanie's stepfather, Michael Cappararo, might have aided in disposing of Bill's car in Atlantic City, and Melanie's friend, Selene Trivizas, might have helped clean the McGuires' apartment after the murder. However, neither was formally charged.

Custody of the McGuires' sons was awarded to Bill's sister, Cindy Ligosh, and Melanie has not seen them since.

CHAPTER 13
THE ALABAMA HATCHET MURDER
FREE BONUS CHAPTER

Huntsville, Alabama, had undergone rapid growth in the decades leading up to 1998, transitioning from a small rural town to an emerging center for the technology and defense industries. The city's population boomed to over 200,000 residents who were drawn in by thriving new employers like NASA and Lockheed Martin. Quiet suburbs sprouted up around Huntsville to accommodate new families looking for that peaceful southern living.

Gerry Franklin had taken an engineering job with a Huntsville defense contractor in the early 1980s when he met Cynthia Drumm, and the two were soon married. As Huntsville continued its evolution into a leading tech hub, dubbing itself "Rocket City," Cynthia took a nursing job at a rehabilitation center.

When Gerry and Cynthia decided to start a family, they purchased a tidy brick home on Camelot Drive in a southeast Huntsville suburb. It was a nice middle-class neighborhood with neatly trimmed lawns—a good place to raise a family. Their first child was born in 1980, a son they named

Jeffrey. Over the next decade, four more children joined the family—daughters Sara and Stacey and younger sons Timothy and Christopher. By the mid-90s, the Franklins were seen as an exemplary Catholic family, with their five children freely playing in the neighborhood while Gerry and Cynthia actively participated in their church and the local community.

The eldest child, Jeffrey, experienced the comfort of a loving family and led a happy, normal childhood. He enjoyed school and sports and had plenty of friends. In middle school, however, his parents noticed when his grades began to slip. From that point forward, the change in Jeffrey was gradual. By age fifteen, he had started to withdraw from friends and family. He quit the school baseball team and gave up playing trumpet in the school band. Jeffrey retreated inward and kept to himself. He often locked himself in his bedroom, blasting heavy metal music and writing privately in his journals.

As Jeffrey's moodiness escalated and his temper shortened, Gerry and Cynthia became increasingly worried. Previously outgoing, Jeffrey now declined family meals and snapped at his siblings.

Alarmed by Jeffrey's mounting anger, his parents began searching for explanations. When they learned of his fixation with the occult and satanism, they turned to church counseling for assistance.

Desperate, his parents sent Jeffrey to a psychiatrist who prescribed him medications for depression and ADHD—Ritalin, Prozac, and Klonopin. Unfortunately, the counseling and pills only seemed to make Jeffrey's behavior worse, not better.

Gerry and Cynthia found themselves with limited options. When exploring the possibility of enrolling him in an intensive treatment program, they encountered a challenge. Due to his age, he was deemed too old for certain programs and not yet eligible for others.

His classmates at Grissom High School could tell something was wrong with Jeffrey Franklin. Long gone was the sweet, intelligent fifteen-year-old. He had changed over the past two years. Now seventeen, he was a completely different person. He was always in a bad mood and seemed to be angry at the entire world. He boasted to classmates about his abuse of Ritalin and how he worshipped the devil.

Cynthia became aware that Jeffrey's supply of Ritalin pills was depleting at a faster rate than anticipated for the prescribed dosage. She eventually realized that Jeffrey had been surreptitiously taking additional pills from the bottle without authorization. It became evident that he had developed an addiction, resorting to abusing Ritalin by consuming multiple pills at once to achieve a high.

Realizing their son faced serious problems, the Franklins were overwhelmed by the severity of his substance abuse and declining mental health. Cynthia and Gerry, feeling powerless, decided that after Jeffrey's upcoming eighteenth birthday, they would arrange for him to be involuntarily admitted to a rehab center. Their only goal was to stop his downward spiral.

Unbeknownst to his parents, Jeffrey had descended into disturbing darkness far worse than they realized. He spent long nights alone in his bedroom, blasting aggressive heavy metal music. By day, he put on a front to keep his family placated. At night, his mental stability spiraled, and he filled notebook after notebook with violent imagery and unsettling writings that revealed a troubled and volatile mental state. He had become undone.

In the late afternoon of March 10, 1998, police responded to a 911 call at the Franklin home. A neighbor had found one of the children on the ground outside the house, lying in a pool of blood. Emergency responders had arrived with only one vehicle, assuming they were responding to only one injured child.

When officers arrived, they were met with a gruesome sight as they approached the home's entrance. Fourteen-year-old Sara Franklin lay across the front threshold, her throat horrifically slashed open and head brutally beaten. Stepping past her battered body, the true scale of the horror awaiting them became gut-wrenchingly clear.

Just inside, the officers came upon the lifeless body of Jeffrey's father, Gerry, surrounded by a sickening pool of blood. His head was left crushed beyond recognition from repeated blows. Nearby lay the murder weapon—a large sledgehammer stained red.

In the hallway, eight-year-old Timothy barely clung to life. His throat had been cut ear to ear, leaving his neck nearly severed. His small head showed severe blunt-force trauma.

In the living room, six-year-old Christopher had suffered similar savage wounds about his throat and head.

Police found a blood-covered hatchet on the living room floor. Jeffrey had used the sharp edge of the hatchet to slash his siblings' throats and the blunt end to viciously beat their heads. Amazingly, the three siblings were still alive.

Upon entering Jeffrey's bedroom, the officers were met with the stabbed and mutilated corpse of his mother, Cynthia Franklin. Her brutalized body lay next to a blood-soaked rattail file—the cause of the horrific puncture wounds covering her body.

The entire house had become an unrestrained slaughterhouse, its rooms turned into nightmarish crime scenes revealing unimaginable violations against human life.

In a small stroke of fortune amidst the bloodshed, eleven-year-old daughter Stacey Franklin had managed to evade the massacre—only because she was at her dance practice when her family was attacked.

Initially uncertain who had attacked the family, detectives questioned a neighbor girl whose disturbing account provided their first break in the case. Fighting through terror and tears, she recalled catching a glimpse of a blood-drenched Jeffrey Franklin leaving the scene.

Huntsville police immediately issued an urgent APB for Jeffrey Franklin and the blue Geo Metro car he was likely driving. It didn't take long for that alert to hit paydirt. A nearby marina guard spotted a shirtless Franklin feverishly rinsing blood off himself and phoned it in. However, realizing he had caught someone's attention, Jeffrey Franklin hastily scrambled back into the Metro and sped away.

When a patrol officer came across a car matching the description, he switched on his lights and sirens in pursuit. The compact Metro's engine screamed as the desperate teen pressed the gas pedal to the floor, the chase now on. More police vehicles soon fell in behind him in what local news stations called a "slow-speed pursuit" as Jeffrey drove through quiet neighborhoods with reckless abandon. During the chase, Jeffrey forced one police car off the road and onto a curb.

The helter-skelter pursuit finally came to an abrupt finish when Jeffrey misjudged his own skill, unable to successfully navigate a sharp corner on a dead-end street. The little Metro careened off the pavement, slamming front-first into a wooden fence.

Jeffrey Franklin didn't resist arrest and was handcuffed without incident. Jeffrey was spotted chuckling and grinning oddly as they took him into custody. Still shirtless, his chest bore scratches in the shape of a pentagram and pitchfork. He gazed at the onlookers with a wild-eyed look of madness and spat at a photographer as he was walked toward the police car. When he spotted a female news reporter, his smile widened further as his tongue unfurled from his mouth, waving and curling in a repulsive manner. An officer said, "Keep it up, funny guy. A jail cell's waiting for you," as he put his hand on top of Jeffrey's head and pushed him into the back of the squad car.

Searching through the gore-splattered home, investigators found a speaker box near the carved-up body of Cynthia Franklin in her son Jeffrey's bedroom. Peering inside the hollow box, they uncovered several notebooks and loose papers crammed with scribbled writings and drawings. The notebooks revealed deeply unsettling insights into the mind behind the massacre.

Across page after page, seventeen-year-old Jeffrey Franklin had composed disturbing writings glorifying satanism, satanic icons, sexual cruelty, and human annihilation. It was clear he had been cultivating morbid fascinations for quite some time.

The journal displayed a chilling intention to snuff out the lives of those closest to him in the most intimate ways. The very weapons and vicious sequences of attack Jeffrey had illustrated on these hidden pages closely matched what officers and paramedics discovered strewn throughout the house. Even the brutal bludgeoning of his unsuspecting father, Gerry, happened precisely as the teenager had penned.

> *I know Dad will be home at this time and I'm going to be, I'll wait by the front door, behind the little hutch, and I'll hit him with a hammer. Mom will be out on a walk, when she comes back, I'll have the radio playing loudly, I'll call Mom in the room and ask her what's on the agenda for today, then I'll kill her, and what about the brothers and sisters. Well, I'll take them, I'll strangle my little brother in his room and I'll lure my other little brother into this room and strangle him. Then my sister, I will rape her then I will finish her off. It's pretty chilling. Even if they do catch me, I will plead insanity, and fool those stupid judges and prosecutors.*

When questioned, Jeffrey Franklin was erratic and acted deranged. He often broke into bizarre laughter and, at other times, became verbally aggressive to investigators. He denied involvement in the attack. He said he was home at the time but didn't attack them. Instead, he said it was like an evil being had taken over his body. That evil being had done the killing—an evil entity that had control over him.

Detectives eventually learned that Jeffrey had been awake for three days straight before the killing, high on Ritalin. He had been snorting three or four pills at a time. His mother had learned that he was stealing the pills and had put them in a lockbox, but Jeffrey had figured out how to take the hinge pins out of the lockbox. He had stolen the Ritalin and replaced them with saccharine pills without his mother noticing. The massive doses of Ritalin had pushed him into total psychosis.

Investigators believed Jeffrey killed his mother first after luring her into his bedroom. He then attacked his sister and waited for his father to come home, attacking him with a sledgehammer as he walked through the front door. Finally, when Jeffrey's two brothers arrived home, he attacked them as well.

Jeffrey Franklin was charged with two counts of murder for the death of his parents and three counts of attempted murder for his siblings. He entered a not-guilty plea and spent three years awaiting trial.

Even though he was seventeen at the time of the murders, the prosecutor was seeking the death penalty. With the amount of writing in his journals, it was clear that he had been planning the murders for quite some time, making an insanity plea difficult for the defense.

Three years later in 2001, knowing there was a good chance he would lose in court, Jeffrey Franklin changed his plea in order to avoid the death penalty. He pleaded guilty to all counts against him and was sentenced to three consecutive life sentences.

While incarcerated, Jeffrey Franklin conveyed regret regarding his offenses and attributed his despicable actions to an intense addiction and abuse of Ritalin, which severely impaired his judgment during that period of his life. This substance abuse, combined with untreated psychological issues, proved to be a toxic recipe.

In August 2022, he was denied parole for the second time.

Online Appendix

Visit my website for additional photos and videos pertaining to the cases in this book:

http://TrueCrimeCaseHistories.com/vol14/

More books by Jason Neal

Looking for more?? I am constantly adding new volumes of True Crime Case Histories. The series **can be read in any order**, and all books are available in paperback, hardcover, and audiobook.

Check out the complete series at:

https://amazon.com/author/jason-neal

All Jason Neal books are also available in **AudioBook format at Audible.com.** Enjoy a **Free Audiobook** when you signup for a 30-Day trial using this link:

https://geni.us/AudibleTrueCrime

As my way of saying "Thank you" for downloading, I'm giving away a FREE True Crime e-book I think you'll enjoy.

https://TrueCrimeCaseHistories.com

Just visit the link above to let me know where to send your free book!

THANK YOU!

Thank you for reading this Volume of True Crime Case Histories. I truly hope you enjoyed it. If you did, I would be sincerely grateful if you would take a few minutes to write a review for me on Amazon using the link below.

https://geni.us/TrueCrime14

I'd also like to encourage you to sign up for my email list for updates, discounts, and freebies on future books! I promise I'll make it worth your while with future freebies.

http://truecrimecasehistories.com

And please take a moment and follow me on Amazon at:

https://amazon.com/author/jason-neal

One last thing. As I mentioned previously, many of the stories in this series were suggested to me by readers like you. I like to feature stories that many true crime fans haven't heard of, so if there's a story that you remember from the past that you haven't seen covered by other true crime sources, please send me any details you can remember, and I will do my best to research it. Or if you'd like to contact me for any other reason, feel free to email me at:

jasonnealbooks@gmail.com

Thanks so much,

Jason Neal

ABOUT THE AUTHOR

Jason Neal is a Best-Selling American True Crime Author living in Hawaii with his Turkish-British wife. Jason started his writing career in the late eighties as a music industry publisher and wrote his first true crime collection in 2019.

As a boy growing up in the eighties just south of Seattle, Jason became interested in true crime stories after hearing the news of the Green River Killer so close to his home. Over the subsequent years, he would read everything he could get his hands on about true crime and serial killers.

As he approached 50, Jason began to assemble stories of the crimes that have fascinated him most throughout his life. He's especially obsessed by cases solved by sheer luck, amazing police work, and groundbreaking technology like early DNA cases and, more recently, reverse genealogy.

- goodreads.com/jasonneal
- bookbub.com/profile/jason-neal
- amazon.com/author/jason-neal
- tiktok.com/@jasonnealbooks
- facebook.com/jasonnealauthor

Printed in Dunstable, United Kingdom